THE JOB SHUFFLE

The Job Shuffle

Douglas Erlandson

MOODY PRESS
CHICAGO

ISBN: 0-8024-4346-X

1 3 5 7 9 10 8 6 4 2

Printed in the United States of America

To my mother, Ann Erlandson,
and my father, the late Gerald Erlandson,
for teaching me to glorify God with my work.

Contents

Acknowledgments

The Job Shuffle would never have seen the light of day had it not been for the help of many people. I certainly cannot mention everyone by name who in one way or another contributed to its development. Many people agreed to be interviewed for this book about their own personal job shuffles and will remain anonymous; to them I simply say "Thank you." In addition, I especially acknowledge the many women who gave me a better understanding of job crises from a woman's perspective.

To the editorial staff at Moody Press I say "Thanks" for reading the manuscript at various stages of development and offering many helpful suggestions. I am sure this book would not have been nearly as good without their help.

Many authors acknowledge the hours spent by their typist deciphering illegible handwriting. My writing *is* illegible. However, because of my Macintosh Classic and Microsoft® Word program, I was able to avoid having to use, and thus burden, a typist. Therefore, I thank the many men and women who made this technology available.

I want to thank my parents for teaching me the value of thrift and hard work and for setting the godly example I have striven to follow. I only regret that my father's sudden departure for Glory this past August prevented his seeing so many of his principles spelled out in print. However, I am confident that he is fully aware of what has transpired.

Thanks to Annie and John, my children, for understanding when I didn't pay as much attention to them as I should.

And thanks to Elizabeth, the wife God has graciously given me. She tirelessly and without complaint read draft after draft of every chapter, helped smooth out my wording, and offered many suggestions for improvement. I thank her especially for her continual encouragement and for believing in me even in the darkest of times. Without her, this book would never have been written.

Above all, thanks be to God for sustaining me through every moment of this venture and for continually answering my prayers for strength and insight. Also, I thank Him that He allows us to continue to live in the Cornhusker State.

Introduction

A job crisis can begin slowly. Dissatisfaction with your job situation can creep in little by little, until you wake up one morning and admit that your present situation is intolerable. Or it can begin all at once. The boss calls you into the office and tells you that your services are no longer needed. Or something happens to totally change your perspective on your work environment.

A job crisis can end in the same way. It may end little by little. Your work situation may change almost without your realizing it. One day it finally hits you that you really love what you're doing and wouldn't want to do anything else. Or it may end quite suddenly. Your phone rings one morning and you're told that you've been hired for that job you wanted more than anything else in the world. All those seemingly fruitless months of applying, all those interminable interviews are now past. You can at last get on with your life, doing what *you* want to do.

I know. I've been through two job crises in my life. The first one began suddenly some fourteen years ago. I received official notification that I wouldn't be granted tenure by the University of Nebraska. Not long afterwards I entered my first period of unemployment. Although I tried all sorts of ingenious ways of making money, nothing seemed to work.

That first job crisis ended just as suddenly—in a sense. In another sense, it continued in a different form. During my nearly three years without a job, I spent my spare time studying for the ministry. When I was licensed to preach and received a call to pastor a church, I thought my long-standing crisis was over. It wasn't. I had a regular paycheck for six years, but I was miscast as a minister. When the second church I pastored turned out to be a "problem congregation," I again began applying for jobs.

I was now in my second job crisis, a crisis that came to a head on a sunny afternoon in early December. I remember the moment vividly. I was sitting on the La-Z-Boy® in the living room of our parsonage. The mail had just arrived and I was skimming a Presbyterian weekly, *The Christian Observer.* On the back page was an advertisement for a public relations writer at Back to the Bible in Lincoln, Nebraska.

I could hardly believe my eyes. A job, a *real* job in Lincoln, Nebraska!

Lincoln—the city where I had spent eight years teaching philosophy.

Lincoln—the city where I had become a Christian.

Lincoln—the city where Elizabeth and I had lived the first two years we were married.

Lincoln—my favorite city. I'd have given my right arm to move back. I had always considered it strange that although I had applied for close to one hundred positions, none had been anywhere near Lincoln. Indeed, not one had been anywhere near Nebraska. But now, all this had changed.

There was only one problem. As I studied the job description, I eliminated myself on all counts. This position needed to be filled by someone else—and I knew just who that person was.

"Elizabeth!" I called into the kitchen. My wife, a budding free-lance writer, came into the room. "Listen to this job listed in the *Observer.*" I read the entire description, up to the point about "Back to the Bible, Lincoln, Nebraska." I paused.

"That sounds like something I could do!" Elizabeth exclaimed.

"I thought so," I responded.

"Where's it located?"

"Guess."

She made several stabs and finally gave up.

"Lincoln, Nebraska!" I said triumphantly.

"No! I don't believe you." Elizabeth grabbed the magazine from me, certain that I was joking. A few seconds later, fully convinced that I wasn't, she said, "I'm going to give them a call."

I'd be an unemployed dad... an able-bodied fellow who stays at home while his wife slaves away at work.

A month and a half later she was offered the job. I now had a full-blown job crisis on my hands. Whereas before I had a job that had become nearly intolerable, now I didn't have *any* job. I'd be *unemployed* when we moved back to Lincoln for Elizabeth's new job. Having been unemployed once before, the very word struck terror in my heart. Worse still, I'd be an unemployed *dad*. We had two young children, and I'd be staying home, taking care of them. I'd be a "Mr. Mom"—an able-bodied fellow who stays at home while his wife slaves away at work. In other words, I'd become an unmotivated, lazy lout.

Nobody puts it quite that way when you're in this situation. After Elizabeth and I set up house in Lincoln, the comments were polite and indirect, yet their meaning was clear: "It's a pity your husband can't find work." "We're praying that he'll get a job." "Has he tried *looking* for work?" "Is he thinking of going back into teaching—or what?"

It's hard to hide, particularly when you have small children in your charge. You're noticed by the man who's repairing your furnace or the plumber who's come to fix your leaky faucet. And, of course, the mother with her children at the playground is extremely curious.

"Does your wife work during the day?

"Yes she does—at Back to the Bible."

"Oh, that's nice. And what do *you* do?" (Meaning, "Where do you work and when?")

How many times I wished I could have said, "I work third shift at Goodyear," or "I teach at the university, but I don't have any classes this afternoon."

Occasionally I'd mutter something like, "I'm a free-lance writer," hoping they wouldn't pry further. Of course, I wouldn't add that my total yearly free-lance income probably wouldn't provide for the family's welfare for more than a month. At least it sounded like I did something for a living.

At other times I'd be brave. "I'm a househusband." Reactions would vary. Sometimes there would be genuine interest and positive reinforcement. More often than not, however, my announcement would be greeted by silence or a quizzical look that said more than a multitude of words.

It was worst among Christians. One evening in particular stands out —Dad's Night at Pioneer Clubs. Since our church didn't have any week-night activities for children, we sent Annie, our oldest, to Pioneer Clubs at another evangelical church. I was sitting across the table from another dad, an especially freshly scrubbed and well-manicured specimen. Somewhere midway through our ice cream sundaes, the dreaded question came: "Where do you work?"

"Well, um—uh—I'm sort of between jobs right now."

A fellow who knew us both was sitting next to me. He came to the "rescue." "Doug used to teach at the university and was a pastor for several years. His wife works for Back to the Bible."

Embarrassed silence. On to other topics.

Yes, I was in an employment crisis. There didn't seem any way out unless I somehow could find a job.

That was more than two years ago. I still haven't found a job. Elizabeth is still working at Back to the Bible. I'm still at home taking care of the kids. But I'm no longer in a job crisis.

One way out of a job crisis is being hired to do a job you really like. Another way out is finding something you really like to do and doing it, even if no one will hire you to do it. I chose the latter alternative. God has graciously allowed me to build up a mail-order business with gross sales of $100,000 a year. I also have another mission—helping others get through and transcend their own job crises.

When we first came back to Lincoln, we felt terribly alone in our predicament. But we weren't. We soon found many others who were struggling with their own job crises.

We heard of a man in Canada who was forced to stay home because of poor health; he looked after the family while his wife went out to work. We found out about another man in Omaha who had opted to stay home with his three-year-old son and do unpaid ministerial work while his wife supported the family. One of my cousins faced long-term unemployment when he lost his job at age fifty.

We really didn't need to look that far from home. In the church we started attending, we found at least half a dozen men, some young, some middle-aged, some near retirement, who were out of work. Others were working but were terribly dissatisfied with their jobs. Not just men, but women too were in this position. Some were working in jobs they didn't like. Others wanted desperately to stay home with their children. Still others were unemployed or had recently gone through a time of unemployment. As Elizabeth and I talked to them, we knew that our situation was not unique.

My curiosity was piqued. Lincoln is a city with an extremely low unemployment rate and a stable work force. Yet, in a very short time, we had encountered scores of men and women who were in an employment crisis. Certainly, I thought, there must be millions nationwide going through the same struggle.

I began doing research. I found out that the number of people struggling with their job situation is actually in the tens of millions. I learned, for example, that the average American will change jobs eight times during his career. According to some estimates, four of five workers are dissatisfied with their jobs. The days of job crises are here to stay.

A job crisis can take several forms—unemployment, job dissatisfaction, reentry into the work force, or some other form of crisis.

People who are going through a job crisis need help. They need you and me to reach out to them. They need the ministry of the church. They need the help of pastors, counselors, advisors. When I was going through my career crises, I could have used this help.

That's why I've written this book. I've written it for people who are going through a job crisis—whether it's an unemployment crisis, a job dissatisfaction crisis, a reentry-into-the-work-force crisis, or some other form of crisis. I've written it for their spouses, their children, their parents. And I've written it for people who want to help—pastors, elders, deacons, counselors, and, of course, friends. You may not be in a job crisis yourself, but you surely know others who are. You need to help.

A major portion of this book is devoted to practical suggestions. Whereas useful, these alone are not sufficient. When a person is going through a job crisis, he is going to question God. Coming to grips with the reality that God has a purpose in what He is doing and ascertaining that purpose are all-important. Part One of this book (chapters 1-3) is designed to aid in this effort. Another major purpose of these chapters is to help those in a job crisis deal with the anger and the anxiety and the loss of self-esteem that often accompany such crises.

Part Two (chapters 4-7) addresses the beginning stages of the job crisis. Part Three (chapters 8-11) deals with how to cope during a job crisis, including how to live without a regular paycheck and how to deal with the effect of job crises on children. Part Four (chapters 12-14) shows you how to *transcend* a job crisis and includes a discussion of your working-at-home potential.

Part Five is addressed to those who may not be going through an employment crisis but who want to help those who are. Chapter 15 shows how individuals can help. Chapter 16 describes the program of Oak Lake Community Church, a church with an active ministry to men and women who are going through job crises.

In an afterword, I address a specific question that arises for families where the husband is at home over a long period of time (perhaps permanently) while the wife is the primary breadwinner: Is this arrangement consistent with the Bible's portrayal of the husband as the head of the house?

The second afterword is written by Elizabeth. In it she addresses the working wives of unemployed men, offering them hope and even joy in their situation.

My hope is that this book will give comfort and help to men and women in job crises, as well as to those who want to help. If it does this, it will have accomplished its purpose.

PART **1**

FACING THE FACTS

1

How It Began

My new Dodge Aspen wagon hummed smoothly as I drove through the night. It was Christmas vacation 1977. I had just finished visiting my brother in Texas and was driving to Chicago to see my parents before heading back to Nebraska. "Blue Bayou" was playing on the radio for about the tenth time. I loved Linda Ronstadt's voice. As I headed up the Missouri Boot Heel in the wee hours of the morning, I was content. However, I couldn't help feeling an occasional touch of anxiety. The philosophy department at the University of Nebraska was making a decision on granting me tenure, and I anticipated finding a letter waiting for me when I reached my destination.

The letter was there, and I was right. The news wasn't good. The department had voted for tenure by the narrowest of margins, not enough for the College of Arts and Sciences to sustain its recommendation. That meant I would soon be looking for another position. Because the job market was very tight, there would be no guarantee I'd find one.

Sure enough, I didn't. And I entered the first employment crisis of my life. No longer would I have the security of knowing that I would receive a paycheck the last day of every month. I would have to find some other way of surviving.

A few months after I heard of the department's tenure decision I became a Christian and almost immediately got involved with a small group in Lincoln that wanted to start a "house of ministry." They faced one major obstacle. They didn't have any money to buy a house. However, their leader convinced me that I would make an ideal pastor and that the other members of the proposed house would be happy to contribute to my financial support.

In retrospect, I have to admit that I was only too eager to believe him. I gave the group $8,000, all I had in my bank account at the time.

With that decision, I began a series of grand mistakes in dealing with my job crisis. Within weeks after the house was purchased, the group made it clear that they had no intention of keeping their promises. With tensions running high on both sides, I moved out of the house. Because nothing had ever been put in writing, I knew that I could kiss that $8,000 good-bye.

By this time I was down to my last few months at the university. My paychecks would soon run out. To replenish some of my savings, I lived as frugally as possible. By the middle of my last semester at Nebraska I had more than $2,500 back in the bank.

That was just enough to purchase a distributorship in a direct sales organization. I offered token resistance before I plunged in. "I'm no salesman," I protested. "The products will sell themselves," I was told. With that assurance, I eagerly gave my new area manager a check for $2,500, got my product from the warehouse, and waited for customers to come flocking my way.

As I drew my last two paychecks from the University, I watched as the "self-selling" lubricants, paints, and cleaning products sat peacefully on my shelves. It dawned on me that the products *wouldn't* sell themselves, that I still didn't want to be a salesman, and that I had better find a different solution to my employment crisis.

Meanwhile, my spiritual life was growing, and I became fascinated with the truths of the Christian life. I enjoyed theology, so I decided to enroll in seminary. However, I didn't give much thought to the long-term financial consequences of this decision either. Had I done so, I may have realized that the two main career paths to which seminary leads are teaching and the ministry. For every teaching vacancy there are hundreds of seminary graduates. And a person needs a special combination of gifts to be fulfilled and effective in the pastorate. Not thinking about what lay beyond seminary, I cashed in what I had built up in my pension fund, paid my first semester's tuition, and headed out to Westminster Theological Seminary in Philadelphia.

Studying theology *was* fascinating. But my studies were soon overshadowed by an unexpected but welcome appearance. I met my beautiful Elizabeth shortly after arriving at Westminster. We got engaged within eight days and were married three months later.

My bride and I had a roof over our heads but absolutely no income. In two weeks of making cold calls, I had one $3.95 sale.

I loved my wife and my God, yet still I had no job and faced tuition payments for a second semester. I knew something had to give. What gave was seminary. Elizabeth and I used part of our remaining cash for our honeymoon and then headed back to Lincoln.

Several years earlier, while still a professor, I had purchased a small, two-bedroom house. Providentially, the Lord had not allowed me to sell this house in the interim. My tenants were former students of mine and good friends. When they knew we were returning to Lincoln, they graciously vacated. So, Elizabeth and I had a roof over our heads but absolutely no income—not even the $250 per month I had been getting from renting my house.

With our bank account dwindling daily, I pulled the products from the shelf and tried to sell them. I found that not only were they not self-selling, but that they resisted being sold even when they were aggressively marketed. After two weeks of making cold calls in Lincoln, I had one $3.95 sale to show for our efforts. We tried our own version of mail order, sending flyers extolling the virtues of our products to all our friends. We made one or two small sales and lost several friends.

We knew a fellow who managed a fairly large apartment complex. From time to time, he hired us to clean and paint vacant units at five dollars an hour. This provided occasional income and gave us some unforgettable experiences—such as trying to clean a bathtub caked with at least four inches of crud.

We soon found another revenue source. I took out my boyhood base-ball-card collection and began selling it piece by piece. I parted with some of my Mantles, Musials, and Aarons at a fraction of their present worth. Providentially, the Lord didn't allow me to sell most of it. Eight years down the road the collection would again come in handy.

Elizabeth eventually got a job working as a secretary for the Animal Control Department in Lincoln. It didn't pay much, but it beat cleaning apartments.

Meanwhile, I tried another business venture. I hung signs all around town advertising "Professional Typing" and tried to compete with my old IBM Selectric against typists with advanced electronic models. Needless to say, my best efforts hardly matched the quality produced by the truly professional typists. Over a period of a year I took in about $1,000. But at least it didn't cost me anything, other than a few dollars in advertising and some time.

At this point, I hadn't given up the hope of finding another teaching job. I applied each time I heard of an opening. I also checked the local want ads, and whenever a job was advertised for which I was even remote-ly qualified, I sent in my résumé. Nothing came up, not even a nibble.

This arrangement, with Elizabeth working and my doing occasional typing, applying for jobs haphazardly, and otherwise puttering around the house, continued for a little over a year. It was then that the pastor of our church suggested that I try to become licensed as a preacher in our denomination.

I was shocked. When I had dropped out of seminary, I thought that I had pretty much cut off this avenue. Our pastor, however, was aware of my ongoing interest in theology and recognized that I had learned much of the seminary curriculum by continuing with independent study after leaving Westminster.

Over the next few months, I studied diligently. Finally I took the li-censing exams and passed them without difficulty. Almost immediately I received a call from a Reformed church in South Dakota. Thinking that my employment crisis was over and that I would again be receiving a regular paycheck, we sold our house in Lincoln and headed to Aberdeen.

We were right about one thing. I received a regular paycheck for nearly six years. But my employment crisis wasn't over. For two and a half years in South Dakota and three and a half in rural Ohio I *endured* the pastorate, all the time wishing I could do something else. I loved God's people. I was an excellent teacher and preacher and a decent administra-tor. As a counselor and comforter, however, I was lousy. And because of my natural shyness and reserve, I felt very awkward trying to make small-talk on pastoral visits and at church potlucks. Many people choose a career without carefully determining whether their talents and interests equip them for what they will be doing. Pastors are no exception.

I may have stuck it out a lot longer had our second congregation not taken an intense disliking to Elizabeth soon after we arrived. To this day I'm not sure just why they did. Perhaps her outgoing, urban personality was too much for them. Perhaps they were offended by her outspoken defense of her Christian principles. Perhaps they just didn't like anyone who was "different." In any case, when their hostility spilled over on our two young children and finally to me, we knew it was time to leave.

Once again I started sending out résumés, this time to literally hundreds of colleges and churches. Although I would have preferred teaching, in my desperation I was even willing to give the pastorate one more shot. Certainly a job would open up somewhere! And, yes, after a year and a half, a job did come up. Unexpectedly, it was for Elizabeth.

Elizabeth hadn't even been looking for work. Almost by accident, I stumbled on an ad for a public relations writer back in Lincoln. I showed it to Elizabeth. She applied, was called for an interview, and was offered the job immediately.

I became unemployed again, a situation I said I would avoid at all costs. My wife again became the family breadwinner.

Now my job crisis began in earnest. As described in the introduction, we jumped at this chance for one of us to work and to return to Lincoln. Nonetheless, we now had to reverse roles once more. I became unemployed again, a predicament I said I would avoid at all costs when I entered the ministry six years earlier. Now after several years of a relatively traditional husband-wife relationship, Elizabeth again became the family breadwinner.

But this time I was more determined to find a means of contributing substantially to the family's financial welfare. Full-time work was out of the question. We had two young children and someone had to care for them. Moreover, I had convinced myself that I was unlikely to find a job much beyond the hamburger-flipping variety.

With nothing to do but look after the children (no small task in itself), I had to find something to keep busy and, I hoped, to make money. I hit on my first business venture quite by accident.

Elizabeth and I knew that her salary alone would not be quite enough to make ends meet. So, to generate some extra cash, I pulled out my baseball cards once again. In the eight years since I had last looked at them, they had increased several fold in value. I figured there might be some demand for them, so I phoned in an ad to the local classifieds. It read: SELLING BASEBALL CARD COLLECTION 1948-1962. MOST NEAR-MINT. I waited to see what would happen.

At 7:30 A.M. the first day the ad ran, I received a phone call. The phone kept ringing the rest of the day, the next day, and the day after that. By the time the classified had run its course, I had made more than $3,000, and I had sold only a small fraction of my collection.

Still, I didn't think of my baseball cards as anything other than a temporary means for generating cash. As the months wore on, however, the business possibilities began to dawn on me. I had already made many local contacts, and I knew that I had only scratched the surface. I reasoned that if I could somehow replenish my supply of cards, I could keep selling indefinitely.

And so I started going to garage sales, hoping to unearth a dusty shoebox full of cardboard gold. I placed a few classifieds, this time offering to *buy* collections. I ran across a few minor bargains, but most of my efforts were hit or miss. Even so, I was replenishing my inventory. More importantly, I was beginning to think of myself as a baseball card dealer.

*A*s I sat at our dining room table, surrounded by boxes of baseball cards, I realized I was no longer unemployed, but self-employed. Almost by accident, I had become an entrepreneur.

Then the first big break came. I had some business cards printed, got a resale tax number, and applied to several major card companies to be put on their dealer list. With the power of buying new cards direct from the factory, I had an advantage over most local collectors. The only hurdle was the rather substantial investment I would have to make to order the quantities the factories required for direct sales.

Providentially, I still had some cash available from the sale of my boyhood cards. I also cashed in some small mutual funds and other investments. This provided enough money to start ordering directly.

But now I needed to find customers to buy the product. Enter the *D&E Baseball Cards Newsletter.* I began mailing this two-page effort to the contacts I had made over the previous months. Each time I made another contact I added his name and address to my mailing list. I used this vehicle to keep everyone informed of my prices on new product as it came out.

I continued to run ads in the classifieds. These provided still more contacts. Finally, when the growth of the business warranted it, I started advertising in national sports collecting publications. Thus began the mail-order wing of D&E Baseball Cards.

And one day, as I sat at our dining room table, surrounded by boxes of cards, knowing that our closets were jammed with cases of inventory, the realization dawned on me—I was no longer unemployed but self-employed. Almost by accident, I had become an entrepreneur.

As with most entrepreneurial efforts, it wasn't all smooth sailing. It still isn't. I experienced, and continue to experience, peaks and valleys. Not all purchasing decisions pay off. Relatively good months alternate with slow months. But the overall trend is one of growth. I praise God for this.

Once the realization hit that I was no longer unemployed and that I was enjoying what I was doing, I came to another conclusion. My job crisis—which had been going on for more than a decade—was over.

Since then I've added another part-time business—freelance writing and editing (also an entrepreneurial endeavor, by the way). The best place to begin writing is with what one is familiar. For me, this was theology and employment crises. (These aren't as far removed from each other as they seem.) Theology was easy to write about (though not especially profitable). After all, I had been studying it for years.

However, my reporting on employment crises required more than just recounting my personal experiences. I had to do some serious research. I read everything I could get my hands on—how to make a successful job search; how to write a better résumé; how to identify your interests and match them to your job; how to start your own business; how to find a career in advertising, real estate, television, or other fields; how to keep from getting fired; what to do when you're fired; how to survive the turbulent nineties; how to change careers after age forty-five; how to live without a paycheck. You name it, I read it.

Among my findings:

- The vast majority of Americans had gone through, were going through, or would soon go through an employment crisis similar to mine.

- Most adults will have three career changes during their working years.
- In any given year, one out of four families will be directly affected by a job change or by unemployment.
- More people than ever will work without a guaranteed paycheck, not only retail shop owners and people who run service business-es, but an increasing number of freelancers of every sort. This dis-ruption will accelerate as we continue to move from an industrial to an informational society. As companies realize the inefficiency of bringing their workers under one roof, many will begin to farm out their work to self-employed individuals in order to save dollars. The age of "telecommuters" working at home will appear.

In the recession-weary 1990s, we have only felt the first tremors of the the coming job disruption. Its enormity is scary but also potentially liberating.

The Christian experiencing unemployment uncertainty has a unique source of security—his faith in a sovereign God who will work all things to his good for the sake of His Son Jesus Christ. Like everyone else the Chris-tian needs to put bread on the table; however, his employment goals should be infused by a desire to bring glory to God and to advance the cause of Christ's kingdom.

The material in this book can be used by anyone, but its principles will especially help Christians cope with their employment crises—and the crises of those with whom they come in contact.

2
Why, God?

For centuries, philosophers and theologians have debated something called *the problem of evil.* They wrestle with a simple yet profound question: "If God is all-good, all-knowing, and all-powerful, why does He permit evil? After all, a good God would want to eliminate evil. An all-knowing, all-powerful God could eliminate evil. Why, then, does evil exist?"

Late-twentieth-century American Christians have their own, down-to-earth problem of evil to deal with. "If God really loves me, why doesn't He give me a secure, well-paying job that I really like for forty-five years? Why do I have to face periods of unemployment or uncertainty?"

"Why do I get stuck in jobs I really hate?" others ask. "Why do I have to make a choice between what I want to do and what my job demands that I do?"

Like its more philosophical cousin, the "job crisis" problem of evil can be resolved only by trusting Scripture's testimony concerning who God is and what He is doing. This testimony is summed up well by the Heidelberg Catechism, which dates from 1563. As part of its answer to the question, "How do you understand the providence of God?" the catechism declares that Providence is "the almighty, everywhere present power of God whereby . . . He upholds . . . all creatures, and so governs them that herbs and grass, rain and drought, fruitful and barren years, meat and drink, health and sickness, riches and poverty, yea, all things come not by chance, but by His Fatherly hand" (Question 27).

That's pretty all-inclusive, isn't it? All things—the bad and the good —come from God's almighty hand. That is why the Heidelberg Catechism can also say of God the Father "that whatever evil He sends upon me in this vale of tears, He will turn to my good; for He is able to do it, being almighty God, and willing also, being a faithful Father" (Question 26).

If this is true—and it's definitely the picture painted by the inspired Scriptures—God has a reason for *everything*, including our times of employment crises. This means that the question, "Why, God?" has an answer.

You may not discern the answer right away. In fact, you probably won't. But as you work through an employment crisis, you will discover two things: first, that God will work many valuable traits into your character; second, that your horizons will be expanded. You will be opened up to possibilities that you would otherwise have missed. In the end, you will thank God for what He has done.

Of course, that depends on your willingness to discern God's sovereign hand. If you refuse, you may see none of this. And your employment crisis will defeat you. But if you approach this time anticipating that God is doing great things for you, you will grow in ways you never imagined. Remember, one of the greatest potential detriments to spiritual growth (and in many cases financial growth as well) is being stuck in the same nine-to-five job for forty-five years. Consider your employment crisis, then, as a special opportunity that God has given you.

Through an employment crisis, God can develop in us certain character traits. Three in particular stand out. They are humility, patience, and trust.

NEW CHARACTER TRAITS

Humility

On our first Sunday back in Lincoln, my family and I had just gotten out of the car in the church parking lot and were hurrying toward the entrance, fighting the sting of the cold March wind. A middle-aged, somewhat overweight man shuffled slowly in front of us. His shoulders were stooped, as though he carried the weight of the world on them. His face brightened momentarily as he greeted us and introduced himself as Ron,* but I could tell from the sadness in his eyes that a long-standing sorrow had settled in his heart.

Because Ron was not accompanied by a woman, I thought that he might have recently lost his wife. Or perhaps he was a lonely bachelor. Maybe he had financial difficulties. But it was none of these.

As the weeks went by and we got to know Ron, his story unfolded. Ron had been a high school principal for nearly twenty-five years. Until he was in his mid-forties he had been a bachelor. Then he fell in love and got married. Not long afterwards, he was driving his new Buick Electra along a country road south of Lincoln. As he reached the crest of a hill, a vehicle traveling at a high speed on the wrong side of the road suddenly loomed in front of him. Ron had no time to react and was hit head on. He escaped with his life, but not much else. A blow to his head affected his memory and his ability to think clearly. Because of a shattered ankle, he was reduced to walking with a severe and permanent limp. Moreover, his wife sued for divorce and "took him to the cleaners."

---

*R*on buried his head in his hands, choked back a sob and said softly yet bluntly, "My self-esteem is ruined."

But perhaps worst of all, he could no longer function as a high school principal, a profession he loved and to which he had devoted his entire adult life. After a while, he had found a low-paying job as a proofreader. While the regular paycheck allowed him to pay his bills, proof-

---

* Although the examples used in this chapter and throughout the book are generally based on the experiences of real people, names and certain specifics have been changed to preserve anonymity.

reading was a sorry substitute for what he really wanted to do. And, although he continued to apply for every principal's job that opened up, it was clear to him and everyone else that he would never be hired.

As I talked to Ron over the next few months, we occasionally discussed this sensitive subject. At first he tried to keep up a somewhat cheerful front, but as I won his confidence, he opened up. His eyes often filled with tears as we talked. One moment in particular stands out. After the church service one Sunday evening, we were conversing in a pew near the back of the sanctuary. Suddenly, Ron buried his head in his hands, choked back a sob and said softly yet bluntly, "My self-esteem is ruined."

Simple, yet poignant words, and ones to which I could relate. I too had felt that loss of self-esteem. It was especially severe each time I received my alumni magazine. When I was a professor, I didn't mind that my former classmates, many of whom I had outshone in college, were advancing in their careers. Once I entered my employment crisis, I could hardly bear to read of all their wonderful accomplishments. Sometimes I might take a quick glance at the alumni news before throwing the magazine away. At other times, I wouldn't even have the heart to look, and the alumni magazine would immediately find its way into the wastebasket.

Even family gatherings became depressing. Thankfully, my family is scattered from coast to coast. Still, I'd occasionally have to talk to my brother, who is the chairman of the department of education at a major university. I'd also see my cousin who's married to an academic dean, and another cousin who's making megabucks as a computer programmer. They all seemed so successful and happy. And I was a miserable failure. *Yes, Ron, my self-esteem is ruined too,* I thought to myself.

Many things can cause a loss of self-esteem. A failed marriage or a debilitating illness are just as harmful as a lost job. However, because so much of our life's energy is invested in our work, an employment crisis, particularly if it results in unemployment or underemployment, may be the greatest blow of all. As women have become more career oriented, this has become as true for them as it has been for men.

However, losing our self-esteem may not be all bad, particularly if our esteem has been of the wrong type. Although the Bible does not use the word *self-esteem*, it has a lot to say about the topic. In fact, the Scriptures recognize two distinct types. Godly self-esteem goes hand in hand with *humility*. Worldly self-esteem is *pride*. To truly cope with an employment crisis, we must not only know the difference between the two, but must seek to attain godly self-esteem while eliminating pride.

The Bible has plenty to say about pride, none of it good. Here are just a few passages:

When pride comes, then comes disgrace, but with humility comes wisdom. (Proverbs 11:2)

Pride goes before destruction, a haughty spirit before a fall. (Proverbs 16:18)

Hear and pay attention, do not be arrogant, for the Lord has spoken. (Jeremiah 13:15)

God opposes the proud but gives grace to the humble. Humble yourselves, therefore, under God's mighty hand, that he may lift you up in due time. (1 Peter 5:5b-6)

Success in a career often leads to pride. Indeed, the career itself can become a god. Sometimes God may choose to throw us into an employment crisis to purge us of this idolatry. We will lose that sense of self-esteem we previously enjoyed, but we will gain humility.

Humility is an attitude that is typically misunderstood and caricatured. So, let's pause a moment.

Humility is *not* walking around with stooped shoulders, eyes on the ground. It's *not* putting on a monk's cowl. Nor is it refusing to accept compliments for a job well done.

Humility *is* knowing that God is in control of your life and that whatever you have accomplished is by the strength He has given you. Humility *is* being able to say with the apostle Paul, "I have learned to be content whatever the circumstances" (Philippians 4:11), and *mean* it. Humility *is* knowing that doing God's will is more important than any earthly accomplishment. Humility *is* knowing that if it's God's will that we are presently unemployed, we are far better off than if we were still drawing a regular paycheck.

Bill, a young man I met a few years back, exemplifies humility. He had been a top-notch linebacker at the University of Nebraska, and a promising career as a professional football player awaited him. Then he tore up his knee. Reconstructive surgery and extensive therapy followed. At first he hoped for a comeback, but it soon became evident that his knee was too badly damaged to ever withstand the rigors of pro football.

"For a long time I felt terrible," Bill says now. "I had really been on an ego trip and loved being the center of attention. But in retrospect, that's just what I needed. God had to knock me down a peg to get my attention."

Today Bill is preparing for a career as a missionary to South America. He exudes confidence once again. However, he knows that whatever he achieves is by the strength that God gives him. Worldly pride led him to idolize himself. Humility caused him to place his confidence in the Lord.

Like Bill, once God has taught us humility, we can have confidence again. This confidence, however, comes not through an unbroken string of successes but because we know that God is in control. And when we know that we are doing *His* will, a new, godly self-esteem will take the place of the old. This form of self-esteem will not vanish when we are thrown into a job crisis. If anything, it will grow as we eagerly wait to see what God is going to do next.

Patience

We live in an impatient society. All you have to do to verify this is observe drivers stuck in rush-hour traffic or heading to the beach on Saturday morning. Or go to a busy supermarket or a bank with long lines at the teller's window. You will soon discover that patience is a virtue we sorely lack.

Americans are especially impatient when it comes to their careers and financial success. We're anxious to get ahead, to move up the corporate ladder, or to become a senior partner in a law firm. We're rarely content with our present salary but want to make more—lots more. And we don't want anything standing in the way of these goals.

Sometimes, however, God stands in the way—mercifully, too, I might add. When our impatience is rewarded, we become all the more impatient. Moreover, we begin to look upon our success as a result of our drive and determination. We forget that whatever success we have comes from the strength that God gives us.

---

*P*atience comes only if we are optimistic concerning the future.... We can be optimistic because we know that God has our situation in His hands.

When we are thrown into an employment crisis, we quickly learn to be patient. The crisis isn't usually resolved in weeks or even months. Sending out our résumés and then waiting, being turned down repeatedly despite promising interviews, watching a new enterprise develop ever so slowly, all build patience. Indeed, a person who doesn't develop a measure of patience will soon crack.

But patience comes *only* if we are optimistic concerning the future. If we become convinced that our job hunt will never succeed, we'll soon abandon it. If we are sure that our new business venture will fail, we'll quickly lose interest. If we don't think we'll find a new career more suitable to our personality, we'll stick it out in our old job, no matter how distasteful it has become.

"How can we be optimistic concerning the future when the present is so bleak?" That's the very question John, an unemployed civil engineer, posed one day. He had sent out résumés for more than ten months and had had several interviews. No job had materialized, and he was back to square one.

Humanly speaking, his situation *was* bleak. But John also knew of a God who controls the future and has promised to work all things to our good. Right there was his answer. We can be optimistic concerning the future because we know that God has our situation in His hands. The One who cares for the birds of the air and the plants of the field (Luke 12:24-28) cares for us as well (1 Peter 5:7). Therefore, we can have patience as we eagerly anticipate how He will work our present situation, no matter how bleak, to our good.

This brings us to the third trait God works in us through an employment crisis—*trust*.

Trust

The psalmist says, "A horse is a vain hope for deliverance; despite all its strength it cannot save. We wait in hope for the Lord; he is our help and our shield. In him our hearts rejoice, for we trust in his holy name" (Psalm 33:17, 20-21). True words, but even for the Christian the temptation to trust in one's "horses" is great.

For most of us, our regular paychecks are our horses. Although Scripture repeatedly commands us to trust in God, we try everything we can to avoid having to do so.

I've always felt better when I've had not only money to pay the bills on time but have been able to save for "a rainy day." That biweekly or monthly paycheck is a great aid to this end. When you know it will be coming in without fail, the temptation to trust it is great.

God sometimes knocks this prop from under us so that we'll have to trust in Him. When we don't know where the money will come from, we have no choice. We either trust in God—or sink into despair.

Trusting God is exciting. More often than not, I've begun a month not knowing whether I'd be making any money and wondering how we would make ends meet. Sometimes whole months are incredibly slow. I don't make the sales I anticipated. Bills come due. New product must be ordered. Everything becomes touch and go. But God has never failed us.

We've always had enough to get by. If I had had a regular paycheck, I doubt I would have noticed God's hand in providing for every need.

If you let Him, God will work each of these virtues in you—*humility*, *patience*, and *trust*.

NEW PLANS

God will also use your employment crisis to open you to new horizons. The possibilities are almost endless. Here are just five ways an employment crisis can lead you into new directions.

Using Your Gifts in New Ways

God may be opening you to new ways to use your gifts and even to discover latent, unused gifts. God gives each of us gifts and talents to use in the service of His kingdom (see 1 Corinthians 12:4-30; Ephesians 4:7-13). Often, though, we underutilize a certain gift or fail to use it at all. When we use our gifts, they develop. When we don't, they atrophy.

Frank was a member of our congregation. Not long after he lost his construction job, he went to see our pastor for counseling. While there, he became fascinated by the parts of an old pipe organ that had been donated to the church but emitted only miserable squeaks. Figuring he might as well spend his time putting together an organ, he undertook its reconstruction. Six months later its beautiful sounds filled the sanctuary.

Jack was an unemployed musician with an interest in electronics. When our church needed a new sound system, he constructed one that was state-of-the-art.

---

*A*n employment crisis may be the nudge you need to assess and test your gifts. Who knows? Maybe you'll discover a hidden gift.

Frank and Jack both eventually found out-of-town jobs in their chosen fields. However, our church is still reaping the fruits of their labor while they were unemployed. As I sit in the pew on Sunday mornings, I can't help but think how God graciously developed in each of them a gift that they may never have discovered if they had been employed in their own professions at the time.

When I left the pastorate I was eager for *any* income I could generate. At first I coauthored a few articles with my wife. Then I began to get fairly regular writing assignments. Before long I found that not only did I enjoy writing, but I could communicate clearly and effectively. While I cannot say with certainty what the Lord would have done, it's likely that had I remained in the pastorate I would not have developed this gift.

An employment crisis may be the nudge you need to assess and test your gifts. Who knows? Maybe you'll discover a hidden gift that you'll be able to use effectively in serving God.

Discovering a New Career

When Don went to college he assumed that a career in insurance awaited him. His dad worked for a large insurance company, and everyone expected him to follow in his father's footsteps. He took all the necessary courses and earned a degree in business administration. After graduation, he went to work in his father's firm as an underwriter. But insurance bored him, and he soon became disenchanted.

Don hoped that he would soon snap out of the doldrums, but the longer he worked, the more he hated it. He could hardly envision another four months behind his desk, much less forty years. When his work began to suffer, he knew it was time for a change.

But what else could he do? He went to a local Christian employment counselor who gave him a battery of tests. As they talked over the results, Don realized that his real love was in counseling people. Don continued to work for the insurance company while he took evening courses in counseling at a nearby college. Once he got his degree, he quit his insurance job and set up practice as a family counselor. Today, ten years later, his practice is flourishing and he is immensely happy in what he is doing.

God may be opening to you a whole new career. Sometimes it requires an employment crisis for us to discover this possibility.

Starting Your Own Business

God may be nudging you to start your own business venture. Being self-employed is at once exciting and scary. It's exciting because you are not beholden to the whims of an employer and are not enslaved to a paycheck. It's scary because the same paycheck you once were enslaved to gave you great security. (This, incidentally, is one of the paradoxes of any earthly form of security. The more security it provides, the more it enslaves us. There are, after all, few people who have more job and life security than the slave.)

Because we are at once enticed and afraid, we tend to procrastinate. Many people would like to begin their own business venture, but few ever do. Or, if they do, their effort is so halfhearted that failure is guaranteed. However, if God wants us to begin this venture, He may give us little choice. Our employment crisis may become so severe that the only option remaining is to take the plunge.

Self-employment is risky, but some day we may look back and thank God for giving us the nudge we needed.

Learning Compassion

God may be equipping you to have compassion on those who are going through "tough times." It's hard to truly understand something you haven't experienced. I can remember as a pastor trying to comfort a young couple who had just lost a baby girl to Sudden Infant Death Syndrome. What could I say—"I know just how you feel"? Hardly. I didn't know how they felt. I could imagine what it would be like to lose my little Annie or John. But imagining sorrow and going through it are like night and day. Thankfully, this couple's faith was strong, and I was able to offer comfort by speaking to them of God's sovereign providence and the hope of eternal life. But even as I did this, I knew that I could not experience the depths of their sorrow.

An employment crisis won't produce the intense sorrow of bereavement. But it can be frustrating, anxiety-producing, even debilitating. A person who hits the turbulent waters of unemployment will quickly understand the loss of self-esteem, the anger, and the pessimism an employment crisis can bring.

Mary had little understanding of or sympathy for the unemployed. A single woman, she had worked for more than twenty years in a local bank and was well-respected by management. She felt she had earned this respect. After all, she was a hard worker with an excellent employment record.

When her bank got taken over by a much larger financial institution, however, she lost her job. She was crushed. Out of desperation she started going to an unemployment support group that met every Thursday evening at the local job service center. She soon realized that other unemployed people were just like her. Often through no fault of their own, they had lost their jobs, and now they were hurting, disappointed, sometimes bitter people, with shattered dreams, hoping that *somehow* they could again piece their lives together.

Mary never did find another job at a bank. Today she works full time with the unemployed and leads a support group at her local church. Her own employment crisis taught her compassion and opened up a whole new career for her.

Adapting a New Lifestyle

To say that Americans are an acquisitive people would be an understatement. We live and work to gain more—more money, more goods, more prestige. And for the most part we live from paycheck to paycheck, spending every dime, often going into debt to obtain our desired lifestyle. The vast majority of Americans are living so close to the edge financially that they are no more than two paychecks away from financial ruin. This generalization applies not only to those who are making $15,000 a year but to those making $50,000 or more.

O f course, you can try to ignore the truth of a financial squeeze. But if you do, you court disaster.

For the most part we continue in blissful ignorance of the impending disaster. When we enter an employment crisis, however, the reality stares us in the face. Through this crisis, God may be making you more open to a new lifestyle.

Of course, you can try to ignore the truth of a financial squeeze. But if you do, you court disaster. Or you can change your lifestyle. You may need to sell that second or third car and put some purchases on hold. You may have to find a different place to live. You may even have to start growing some of your own food, baking your own bread, sewing your own clothes. In a word, you will have to start scaling down.

But the end result may be something far better than you ever imagined. The simpler lifestyle will prove less hectic. You will learn to appreciate what you have. And when God places your financial feet under you again, you will find that you have much more discretionary income than you ever imagined, income that you will be able to use for God's work on earth.

God may even be using your employment crisis in ways very different from any of these. But one thing of which you can be sure—if you are open to the leading of God, He will expand your horizons during this time.

An employment crisis can be frightening, anxiety-producing, even debilitating. But if you approach it with the right attitude, trusting that your sovereign God will see you through, it can be one of the most challenging, exciting periods of your life.

3
God is Faithful

*C*heryl heard the familiar sound of Tom's car pulling into the drive. *Right on time tonight*, she thought as she went to the door to greet him. *We'll get supper finished early.*

As soon as she saw him, she could tell something was wrong. "Wh—what's the matter, honey?" she stammered.

"Lost my job," he replied angrily, as he brushed past her and headed toward the bedroom.

"What? What do you mean?" Cheryl called after him. But Tom had already headed down the hall. The sound of the bedroom door slamming shut drowned out her words.

No sense in getting him any angrier. I'll wait for him to come out, she thought.

Nevertheless, those curt, chilling words frightened her. Did Tom get fired? Or was he just laid off? If so, for how long? How long would they be able to keep up the mortgage payments? And what about Jennifer and Sarah? Did this mean they would have to pull their daughters out of the Christian school? All these questions raced through Cheryl's mind as she nervously puttered around the kitchen, setting the table, checking the roast, and putting the potatoes into the microwave to bake.

When Tom finally reappeared, he seemed calmer. Wrapping his tall, thin frame around the kitchen chair, he began telling Cheryl what had happened. His voice betrayed little emotion, though Cheryl knew he was unsettled. His company, a major defense contractor, had been gradually losing business because of the cutback in military spending, he explained. "Management finally decided to let more than 1,000 employees go. They said it was a painful decision for them, but it's not like *our* pain. I've been with them twelve years, and I get to be one of the 1,000."

Cheryl embraced her husband, and her mind began to whirl. *How could they do this to Tom? He's been a good, faithful employee.* Tears welled up in her eyes—tears of anger. *How could they do this? How could God let this happen?*

Later that evening, after putting the children to bed, Tom and Cheryl sat in the family room, trying to sort things out. They discussed how they could maintain the budget, where they would have to cut back, whether Tom had much chance of getting another job, whether Cheryl should go back to work. But most of all they expressed their anger and frustration —at their situation, at Tom's firm, and at God.

In another part of town, Fred and Brenda Twilling enjoyed bringing in two incomes. Fred was a skilled pastry chef in a local hotel restaurant; Brenda wrote copy for an ad agency. Because neither job paid very much, they felt they both needed to work, not just to make ends meet, but to build up a little cushion if and when they started a family.

Having a family, however, seemed to be a far-off dream. Brenda had fertility problems, and although they were on the waiting list of several adoption agencies, they held out slight hope of getting a baby this way.

Then the family came—and grew. First they heard from the adoption agency. They were about to get a child. And then, one month later, Brenda found out that she was pregnant. They were delighted, though they took a lot of good-natured ribbing from the other young couples in their church. And everyone had a good laugh when the assistant pastor, at the annual church banquet, dubbed them the "Twice-Blessed Twillings."

But for Fred and Brenda a dilemma arose. Brenda desperately wanted to stay home with her children. Fred agreed; he disliked the thought of day care. They had always dreamed that some day they would have a family and that Brenda would care for the children. Now that their dream was about to materialize, however, they were scared. How could they possibly survive without Brenda's salary? How could they feed two more mouths? And wouldn't they have to find a larger apartment, now that they had a family?

Anger and *anxiety.* These are two common reactions when a person is confronted with an employment crisis. They're natural reactions, and we would like to think that they're justified.

But let's pause for a moment. Are they really justified? After all, with whom are we angry?

With ourselves? Maybe so. Sometimes we're right to blame ourselves, such as when we're fired for our misconduct. But more often than not, our job crisis has come about because of circumstances beyond our control.

Tom and Cheryl wanted to blame Tom's firm. They had lost their defense contracts and were taking it out on Tom. But the company had no control over the government's defense cutbacks. And given the easing of world tensions, the government was justified in cutting back on military spending.

Who, then, has brought about the job crisis? Ultimately, God. If we're angry with our circumstances, the One with whom we're angry is God.

And what about the anxiety we feel? Why are we anxious?

Several years ago I saw a sign outside a church: "Anxiety is a mild form of atheism." I couldn't have said it better myself. The only thing I'm not so sure about is just how mild a form of atheism anxiety is.

---

he first step toward coping with a job crisis is to overcome our anger and anxiety. But we can do this only if we believe that God is in control and that He is faithful.

Think for a moment. What causes anxiety? Fear, particularly fear of the future. From our perspective, the future is uncertain. We don't know for sure whether we will have a roof over our heads next year, whether we will have enough to eat, clothes to keep us warm, or money for our children's education. We rightly fear the future if the future is a product of blind chance. If God controls the future, we have no reason to be afraid. Anxiety bespeaks a lack of trust in God.

Now, I don't want to leave the impression that when "real Christians" face an employment crisis they won't have these reactions. They will. Tom and Cheryl did. Fred and Brenda did. Elizabeth and I did, too.

The first few months I was home taking care of the children, I often felt angry. Why should I, of all people, be forced to change diapers, cook meals, do the laundry, and face the embarrassment of having to tell people I didn't have a job? Time and again anxiety washed over us as we wondered whether Elizabeth's paycheck would cover our monthly bills, as we put off getting dental check-ups and buying new shoes for the kids, and when we thought for sure I would never find work.

Eventually, though, anger and anxiety must be put aside. Such reactions will destroy us. Anger will turn to bitterness, anxiety to paralysis.

The first step, then, toward truly coping with a job crisis is to overcome our anger and anxiety. But we can do this only if we believe that God is in control and that He is faithful.

Remember the answer to Question 26 of the Heidelberg Catechism? It says of God the Father "that whatever evil He sends upon me in this vale of tears He will turn to my good, for He is able to do it, being almighty God, and willing also, being a faithful Father."

He is *able* and *willing*. This is the sort of God that Scripture reveals to us. The psalmist says of God that "He determines the number of the stars and calls them each by name. Great is our Lord and mighty in power; his understanding has no limits" (Psalm 147:4-5). And the prophet Isaiah declares, "I am the LORD, and there is no other. I form the light and create darkness, I bring prosperity and create disaster; I, the LORD, do all these things" (Isaiah 45:6b-7).

If God has determined the course of the heavenly beings, if He has formed light and darkness, if He controls wealth and poverty, surely He can take each one of us through our times of economic crisis. He is *able* to do it, being almighty God.

During His earthly ministry, Jesus told His followers: "Are not two sparrows sold for a penny? Yet not one of them will fall to the ground apart from the will of your Father. And even the very hairs of your head are all numbered. So don't be afraid; you are worth more than many sparrows" (Matthew 10:29-30). Our God is involved with the intimate details of our lives. Because He is, Jesus can also say: "So do not worry, saying, 'What shall we eat?' or 'What shall we drink?' or 'What shall we wear?' For the pagans run after these things, and your heavenly Father knows that you need them. But seek first his kingdom and his righteousness, and all these things will be given to you as well" (Matthew 6:31-33).

If God has numbered the hairs of our head, if He has promised to provide for our daily needs, we can trust Him to take us through every economic crisis. He is *willing* to do it, being a faithful Father.

Having memorized the Heidelberg Catechism and having taught it to youngsters year after year as a pastor in a Reformed church, I believed the words of its answer to Question 26. But I didn't know how true they were until I saw how faithfully He provided when I had no way of providing for myself and my family. And what I found true, others have as well.

Look at the ways three couples responded to their job crises. Jim and Kellie were a young couple in the church we started attending after we moved to Lincoln. Jim had been a music major in college. After graduation, he found a job working nights at the local Goodyear plant. It was hard and unrewarding work. But he was thankful he had a job to tide him and his wife over until he could build his reputation as a performing artist. But a year after being hired, he got the news—Goodyear would be laying off workers. Lacking seniority, Jim was one of the first to go.

Jim was angry and, as he puts it, "terrified." But, he also acknowledges, "God provided. It wasn't always easy—especially at first. We sold the car Kellie brought into the marriage. We put some purchases on hold. And we had to cut out all 'extras' for awhile. But little by little God showed us His faithfulness. Kellie got a job working for the city. And I made some money playing the organ and giving music lessons. Finally, I landed a job as a substitute teacher. We're still not rich, but as I look back, I can't point to a time when we didn't have enough to eat or a roof over our heads."

Gene and Fern were much older when unemployment hit. Gene had been a vice president in a small but prosperous firm that had been taken over by a much larger competitor. The merger cost him his job. Now in his midfifties, he was out of work. At his age, he was close to being unemployable.

Providentially, Gene and Fern had always lived well within their means. Their home was paid for, and they had built up a sizeable nest egg. Moreover, their children were all grown and on their own. Still, this did not serve to diminish their anger.

"We were both angry—angry at being treated so shabbily, and, yes, angry at God," Fern admits. "But then we got to thinking. Why should we be mad at God? All those years we were paying off our mortgage, staying out of debt and saving, God's hand was leading us. He was faithfully providing so we would be prepared for this day."

If anyone had the right to be angry, it was Annette. Three years ago she was working in a well-paying job as an office manager. The only thing she didn't like was being tied down from nine to five every day of the week. When she heard about a job in another company that offered a flexible schedule and an opportunity to travel, she jumped at the chance to apply. When she got the job, she was elated. Eight months later her new firm went under.

---

*A*nnette was out of work. . . . "I was mad . . . at the company that went out of business . . . at all the places that refused to hire me. And sometimes I was just plain mad at God."

Annette was out of work. What was worse, shortly afterwards she had emergency surgery. Her savings were soon exhausted, and she was stuck with thousands of dollars of unpaid medical bills. She applied for another job with her old company but with no success. In fact, no matter how feverishly she looked for work, the doors always seemed to be closed.

"I was desperate," she admits today. "And I was *mad.* I didn't really know who to be mad at. Sometimes I was mad at myself for not being content in the first place. Sometimes I was mad at the company that went out of business. Sometimes I was mad at all the places that refused to hire me. And sometimes I was just plain mad at God."

When she had no place else to turn, Annette started attending church again. One evening she went to an adult singles Bible study. That's where she met Bob, a recovering alcoholic and drug addict. Bob's wife had divorced him because of his addictions and had long since remarried. He was terribly lonely, but at least he had a stable job. Annette and Bob hit it off right away. Within months they were married.

"I guess we were both pretty sorry cases," says Annette. "I was broke. Bob had been through hell with his chemical dependency and failed marriage. But it's all worked out well. Just think! If I had found another job right away, I probably wouldn't be back in the church today, and I most certainly wouldn't have met Bob. Given what I have today, I thank God for closing most of the doors I was banging on."

Circumstances still aren't perfect for Jim and Kellie, for Gene and Fern, and for Annette. Each of them still faces many uncertainties. But that's the way life is. Our future is uncertain. And when we are facing an employment crisis the future seems especially uncertain.

Anger and anxiety are natural reactions. But we can deal with them in one of two ways. Doubting God's promise to work all things to our good

(Romans 8:28), we can let them continue to grow. If we do this, they will overwhelm us. Eventually, we will drown in a sea of despair.

Or we can accept God's promise. Like Jim and Kellie, Gene and Fern, and Annette, we will then be able to discern the mighty hand of our heavenly Father turning all adversity to our good. When we trust in the One who is *able* and *willing*, we can rid ourselves of all anger and anxiety.

PART 2
GETTING READY TO SHUFFLE

4
I'm Going to Lose My Job— What Should I Do?

*B*arry Holman was head of the marketing department at General Digital, a midsized electronics manufacturer in a large Midwestern city. He thought his job was secure until he heard about a takeover bid by a much larger company. Realizing his days might be numbered, Barry began looking for another job. He studied the want ads in the Sunday paper, contacted his network of friends, letting them know he was looking for work, and even visited an employment agency. Several viable leads turned into interviews. Because he was still employed, he had to take time off for this purpose. However, he had accumulated several extra vacation days, and he drew on these. Within three months, Barry was hired by another firm. His decision to leave proved wise. General Digital was taken over, and most of its employees got axed.

This included Mark Carey, Barry's close friend and General Digital's comptroller. Barry and Mark were both members of the same church, and their families frequently went on outings together. When Barry found out about the takeover bid, he immediately told Mark. Mark's attitude was that there was nothing to fear because, as he put it, "General Digital will surely protect its loyal employees." Barry reasoned with Mark that the new firm already had a comptroller and would not need another one. But nothing shook Mark's confidence that his job was secure. Only when he found out that he was being terminated in two weeks did he believe otherwise.

Occasionally a person loses his or her job suddenly and without warning. Much more frequently, however, the warning signs are there. Have you heard that your company may be bought out by a larger firm? Does it look like your department is going to be phased out? Is there an industry-wide downturn? Has your supervisor's attitude toward you changed significantly? All these may be indications that you will soon lose your job. *Start preparing now.*

Remember, it's much better to err on the side of caution. If you're prepared for termination and your job is secure after all, you're in the driver's seat. You can always turn down a new job if one is offered. Or you can take it if it's better than the one you have now. However, if you're not prepared and your job is terminated, you're out of work. Heed the warning signs and be prepared.

What if you're one of those individuals whose termination has come without *any* warning? Although rare, this happens. And sometimes employers act on irrational whims. Or perhaps the warning signs were too subtle for you to discern. My advice is the same. *Prepare and act today.* Maybe you have been given only two weeks' notice or a month's severance pay. Start acting at the beginning of those two weeks or that month, not at the end.

All this may seem too obvious to need stating. It isn't. Like Mark Carey, most people don't want to face unpleasant possibilities. They would rather bury their heads in the sand and hope that somehow everything will work out. As a result, they lose whatever precious time they have. (When facing unemployment, time is precious, whether it's two weeks or six months.)

Prepare. How? To prepare you need to follow the "Four Steps of Preparation for Unemployment." They are pray, consider your options, get ready, and plan financially.

PRAY

You may be thinking, "Hey, of course I'm going to pray." Too often, however, prayer is the last thing we think of in times of crisis. Or our prayers are extremely general and little more than an extension of wishful thinking: "God, please make everything turn out all right"; or, "God, make sure I get another job"; or, "God, make my boss relent"; or, "God, please don't let them lay off any workers." You can pray these prayers if you want. They probably won't be particularly effective.

If you're facing unemployment, you're entering one of the most crucial times of your life. You'll need God's specific guidance as you consider your options, as you get ready to find another way of making a living, and as you plan financially. If you're really serious about praying through this time, you will discover that your prayers will become very specific. ("God, please guide me in deciding whether to include on my résumé my reasons for leaving Universal Widget ten years ago.")

Remember the promise of Scripture: "The prayer of a righteous man is powerful and effective" (James 5:16). That promise is for all times—including unemployment.

CONSIDER YOUR OPTIONS

Before you take specific action you need to know your options. You may have several.

First, your spouse could look for work. This option is not open to single people, including single parents. Nor will you consider it viable if your spouse already works and you are convinced you need two incomes to make ends meet. Before you rule out this possibility on these grounds, however, read chapter 6 on downscaling your lifestyle.

If you are a husband facing unemployment, you may be adamantly opposed to your wife replacing you as the breadwinner. You may even have scriptural grounds for rejecting this as a long-term solution. (See Afterword 1 for a discussion of what the Bible says about this arrangement.) However, you may not find a job right away. It is certainly prudent for your wife to start looking for work as soon as you realize your job is in jeopardy —even if you are determined that this will only be a temporary solution. (If your wife starts looking for work, she too should read this chapter. The suggestions for job seekers will apply to her as well.)

Self-employment is a second option. Your initial reaction may be to consider this especially attractive, particularly if you are fed up with "the system" after having lost your job several times before or if this is your first time and you have no idea how to look for work. You may also think of this as an option if you envision yourself as a risk-taker. Before you look seriously at this alternative, read chapter 13 on the benefits and pitfalls of self-employment.

Third, you may decide to retire and live off your investments. Admittedly, this is a viable option for only a few. However, if you are independently wealthy or have squirreled away your money for many years, you may be in this position. (I know of one man in his thirties who inherited enough money to live comfortably off the interest. He quit his job so he could be home to help rear his family.)

If you have the resources, pray about this alternative. But don't think of this as an opportunity to live a life of ease. God calls us to constructive work. But not all work pays money. This may be your opportunity to do volunteer work or to serve your church full time in an unpaid capacity.

Finally, you may decide to look for another job. At this point you will be confronted by another crucial decision. Are you going to look for work in your present field or is this the time to change careers? Most of the advice I will be giving in the remainder of this chapter is applicable to both types of job-seekers. However, if you are even remotely contemplating a career change, read chapters 5 and 12.

Once you've decided on an option, you're ready for the next step.

GET READY

If you've decided on self-employment, read chapter 13. I have only one suggestion to add at this point. *Get started now.* You will not earn a lot of money the first six months to two years. Whether you go into sales, become a consultant or a freelancer, or start your own business, the financial going will be slow at first. However, the more you do at the start, the more you will benefit further on. If you're still employed, whether you have two weeks or six months until termination, *now* is the time to start making contacts. These will pay off when you no longer have a paycheck and really need the money. If you're already out of work, you still should begin immediately. The sooner you start, the sooner your business may take off (or the sooner you may locate a job). That is much better than waiting one year before even starting. So, even if you need to sacrifice evenings and Saturdays, begin now.

If you've decided that you or your spouse must look for work, here is what you need to do. (Again, start doing this today.)

Get Your Résumé in Order

It is possible to get a job without a résumé. However, your chances are broadened immeasurably if you have a résumé to send to a prospective employer. In fact, it's almost necessary as the first means of contact with a firm where you don't already have an "in." (Even if you get a job interview as a result of simply filling out an employment application, having a résumé available will give your prospective employer much more data with which to evaluate you.)

If you haven't had to look for a job for several years, you may not have any idea how to construct a résumé. I would suggest that you look at the sample résumés that are frequently found in books on employment counseling. (I've included a list of several useful books at the end of this chapter.) You will find that some of these writers have strong opinions on what a good résumé should look like. Others don't. You will get some useful advice and these samples may prove helpful as you construct your own résumé. But you will also be thoroughly confused if you try to follow *all* their advice.

I believe the really important advice can be given in several simply stated points.

- The chronological résumé (one which lists your employment history by job with the most recent job first) is preferable in most cases to the functional résumé, which emphasizes your abilities and accomplishments. The functional résumé shows your functional capacities first, and it notes your work history at the end. The functional résumé *may* be preferable for people changing careers and first-time job seekers, and probably is the best alternative for a person reentering the work force after an absence of many years (such as a homemaker).
- Résumés *must* be neatly typed, without grammar or spelling errors. If you are unsure of your abilities in any of these areas, find someone (such as your spouse or a friend) who can help you.
- Your résumé should not look cluttered. Make sure there's enough white space to make it easy to read. Also, make sure those things you want to highlight stand out clearly.
- If you are applying for more than one type of job (for example, accountant and financial analyst), construct a separate résumé for each. This will allow you to emphasize skills and achievements relevant to that particular type of job. Construct a special résumé for any *specific* job in which you are especially interested and for which you are well qualified. (All this takes work, but it's worth the effort. If you have access to a word processor, the additional work is minimal.)
- Stating your career objective is optional. The big drawback is that it restricts the variety of jobs to which you can apply. This drawback, however, is eliminated if you are willing to construct several different résumés.

Rules for the Right Résumé

Here are ten rules for a strong, appealing résumé that should attract the attention of the personnel department or other preliminary reviewer:

1. Prepare a chronological résumé (most recent job listed first) instead of a functional résumé. A functional version is helpful only if you are changing careers or are a first-time or reentering job-seeker.
2. Type the résumé neatly, without grammar, spelling, or typographical errors.
3. Include wide margins and enough white space for a legible, uncluttered look.
4. Prepare a separate résumé for each type of job you are seeking. This will allow you to emphasize skills and achievements relevant to that particular job opening.
5. Limit the length to a maximum of three pages. One page is ideal for attracting the attention of the busy job recruiter.
6. Include your name, address, and telephone number on the résumé. Personal data, such as your health, is optional.
7. Account for all gaps in your employment history.
8. Never lie on your résumé.
9. Emphasize your strengths and achievements. The résumé should be positive; you do not need to indicate your reason for leaving a previous job.
10. A salary history is optional, though including it may rule you out by an employer who cannot match your current salary.

- Your résumé should be long enough to say everything that needs to be said *and no longer.* Ideally, this can be done in one page. If it requires three pages, that's also acceptable. (However, make sure that what's on page one *grabs* the reader's attention.) If it takes more than three pages, you're either one of the most talented and successful people around or you've included nonessentials. Ask yourself, "Is this information relevant to my getting a job?" As a rule of thumb, if it is, add it. If it's not, keep it out.
- Your name, address, and telephone number should appear on your résumé, either at the very beginning or at the end, where it is easy to find. (If you choose to leave your address and telephone number

until the end, make sure your name is found at the top of page one.)

- Personal data is optional—very optional. Your prospective employer probably does not care *where* you were born, and he or she cannot legally ask *when* you were born. Everyone's "résumé health" is always "good" or "excellent." Adding this will not impress anyone. Stating church membership is OK if you're applying for jobs where you think it will help. Your prospective boss probably doesn't care about your hobbies, unless the skills they require will be used in your new job. You don't need to mention that you're married and have five kids, unless you feel that it adds to your image of stability. (However, it may also make your prospective employer think you'll be less willing to travel.) Again, the rule of thumb: If it will help, keep it in. If not, keep it out.

- Account for all gaps in employment history. If you left a job to go back to school or to enter the military or to stay home with the kids, make sure that this is evident to anyone reading your résumé. Unexplained gaps make an employer suspect that you may be hiding something.

- *Never* lie on your résumé. Not only is lying a violation of God's ninth commandment, but it is extremely imprudent as well. Employers do check up on résumés. You will be immediately eliminated from further consideration for a job if your prospective boss finds out that you've lied.

- A résumé can and should emphasize the positive about you. After all, you *are* advertising yourself through your résumé. You should list your strengths and your achievements. You don't have to list your weaknesses or your failures. At the same time, you shouldn't "puff" your résumé with misleading claims. You may have been president and CEO of the Widget Corporation, but if the Widget Corporation was a one-person operation, stating your title in this way is highly misleading.

- A salary history is optional. Your prospective employer won't eliminate you if you don't have this on your résumé. If he's really interested, he'll ask. You can provide these figures then. I would say that unless you're *unwilling* to work for less than you're making now, don't include it. An employer who can't match your current salary (or your salary in your most recent job) isn't likely to consider you a viable candidate.

- Stating the reasons for leaving previous jobs is optional. Some employment counselors say that you should, others that you shouldn't.

If your reasons are suspect (for instance, "I couldn't stand my boss's office clothing") or bizarre ("Everyone else was shot in a hold-up and the place went out of business"), leave them off.

- Beware of résumé services. Some of them are simply résumé *typing* services. They won't provide any real help in *constructing* your résumé. On the other hand, résumé services that take your employment data and actually *prepare* a résumé are expensive. Moreover, they tend to follow a formula. While your résumé will look neat and appear very professional, it will be nearly indistinguishable from hundreds of others these services have prepared. My feeling is that with time and effort you can do as good a job yourself and will have a résumé that truly displays your strongest qualities.

- Finally, have someone carefully read your résumé. Have this person check for grammar and spelling, and then have him tell you in his own words what your résumé says. If it doesn't communicate to him, it won't mean much to a prospective employer either.

In addition to your résumé, you will need to know how to write cover letters for the jobs for which you apply. These should be brief and should highlight a couple of the most salient points on your résumé. Several of the books listed at the end of this chapter have sample cover letters.

Check the Want Ads

Once you have prepared your résumé, the next step is to look at the want ads in the local newspapers. Begin this while you are still preparing your résumé. (Otherwise, you may lose out on some good opportunities.) Check your local paper daily, but particularly its Sunday edition. If you don't mind making a geographical move, study the want ads in the Sunday editions of major out-of-town papers. (These are usually available through the public library.)

See "Using the Help Wanted Ads" (next page) for suggestions and cautions in using your newspaper classified section for finding a job.

In addition to want ads in your paper, check periodicals such as the *National Business Employment Weekly.* And don't forget the professional journals in your field. Many of these list employment opportunities. While they will not have the sheer number of ads found in the newspaper, they will contain a much higher percentage applicable to your skills.

Significantly, only 20 to 25 percent of all jobs are listed in the newspaper classified section. This means that to broaden your job search as much as possible, you will need to do more than just respond to want ads.

Using the "Help Wanted" Ads

Your daily newspaper carries an entire section of "help wanted" classified advertising, even more in its Sunday edition. Here are some suggestions to use this resource effectively during your job search.

1. Apply for a job for which you are qualified. Skip those where you lack the specific qualifications listed. However, don't rule out a job just because you don't fit all the listed qualifications perfectly. An employer whose list is long and specific may never find the perfect fit. Carefully evaluate each ad to determine whether you *possibly* qualify. If you do, apply.

2. Remember skills you have acquired somewhere other than on the job or through formal education. Perhaps you haven't had "three years experience in a management capacity." But you may have gained management skills through your service on the PTA board. You may not have been employed as a computer operator, but you may have gained considerable experience by working with your home computer. (This advice is especially important for people who are reentering the work force for the first time in many years.)

3. Be suspicious of ads that promise you the world. "Earn big bucks—Set your own schedule" or "Join our sales team—unlimited earning potential" sound too good to be true. Often they are. Many of these are direct sales organizations or other operations that require you to build up your own business from scratch. Eventually you may earn big dollars, but it will take time.

4. Don't rule out ads with a blind post office box number, but be suspicious. Reputable companies generally don't mind putting their names in their ads. Also, it's possible that an employer has put in an ad just to see which of his employees are looking elsewhere. (If you know you are about to lose your job, this last consideration is irrelevant.)

5. Many want ads are genuine openings, but not all are. Some organizations want to hire someone from within and put an ad in the paper only to show that they have conducted a public search. The problem is that there is no surefire way to determine this from the ad itself.

Consider an Employment Agency

An employment agency can be a strong resource. But before you register with such an organization, be careful—not all employment agencies are created equal. Some will do little more than let you know of the existence of a few jobs for which you *may* be qualified.

Learn as much as you can about an employment agency before using it. Check with your friends. Some of them will have gone through employment agencies. Which ones did they like? Which ones were unsatisfactory? Why? The recommendations of your friends are your best way of initially screening employment agencies.

Once you make your first direct contact with an employment agency, find out what they do for you. If they offer you a contract, read it carefully. Make sure that the employment agency will really work to get you a job. Otherwise, don't use it.

(My personal feeling on using employment agencies is that if you're willing to conduct an aggressive job search on your own, they are superfluous. However, if you're not, they may be of some value—provided they make a genuine effort to place you.)

Discover Jobs Through Networking

Consider using the contacts your friends have to learn of job openings. This is known as *networking*. Your most important step in looking for a job may be networking. Only 25 percent of jobs are advertised. Employment agencies don't know of all the others, by any means. Your best source of leads may be your friends. Start contacting them now. Let them know you are looking. Ask them to keep an eye out for potential openings. If they don't know of any openings, ask them if they know of someone who might. Contact that person. Give them copies of your résumé to pass on to others. Keep expanding your network. The more people you have working for you, the better.

You may think you're too shy to do this. You may even find it humiliating to tell others you need a job. Being a shy person myself, I can empathize with you. However, if you don't do any networking, you're going to immediately eliminate one important source of job leads. I suggest that you start with those you feel most comfortable with—your best friends, perhaps your relatives. This will help build up your confidence.

When you realize that most people genuinely want to help, you will start losing your fear of contacting them. You may never be an aggressive networker, but you will get better. The better you get, the more chance you'll have at job leads.

Learn How to Have a Successful Interview

Many people prepare beautiful résumés, diligently answer want ads, contact employment agencies, and build up a network of friends. Unfortunately, they don't prepare for the interview. Before an employer hires you, he will certainly interview you. If you don't have an impressive interview, your other preparation will go to waste.

Before the interview, find out everything you can about the company with which you're interviewing. If you know someone who works there, talk to him. If the company has public-relations material, obtain it. Find out what they make, what they do, what their corporate philosophy is. The more you know, the better. If possible, find out in advance who will be interviewing you. If you know someone in the company, ask him what the person interviewing you is like.

Dress appropriately for the interview. This is *not* the time to wear your green blazer and white pants. Forget the tie with the picture of a Hawaiian sunset. Men should wear a conservative blue or black suit, white shirt, a subdued tie, black shoes and socks. Women should wear a dress suit with a plain blouse. Jewelry and make-up may be worn in moderation. Don't wear large earrings or bracelets. In addition, make sure your breath is fresh for the interview. Avoid excessive cologne or perfume.

The interviewer may take you to lunch, with the interview occurring during or after a nice meal. Though the setting may be elegant, order something that is easy—and inexpensive—to eat. This is not the time for crab legs or oysters, even if they are the menu item that most appeals to you. If you're being interviewed by a Christian organization, you probably won't face the issue of ordering an alcoholic beverage. If you're not, the interviewer may order a drink. Decline, even if you're not a teetotaler. (You need your senses as sharp as they can be.)

After the interview, write a thank you note. This common courtesy is often ignored. More than one person, however, has been hired because he or she was the only candidate to remember to do this. The thank you note is also a perfect opportunity to reiterate some point you want to emphasize or to highlight a positive qualification. It's also appropriate to let your prospective employer know that your enthusiasm for the job has increased. (If you've decided the job is not for you, still write a thank you note to be polite. In this case, however, there's no reason to elaborate on a simple "thank you.")

For a listing of style and other preparation pointers for the interview, see "Getting to Know You" on the next page.

Getting to Know You

The interview with your potential employer is the final, and sometimes most frightening, part of the job search. The interviewer is sizing you up—evaluating your appearance, your personality, and your responses. Here are seven tips for letting the interviewer know the true you, and for your being natural and prepared.

1. *Be on time.* This means that you must plan to arrive early. You need to allow time for the unexpected—getting lost on your way to the interview, slow traffic, trouble finding parking, a slow elevator. If you don't encounter any snafus, you can use the extra time to mentally prepare yourself.
2. *Watch your posture.* Sit straight in the chair. Leaning too far forward is associated with aggressiveness. Sitting with your arms folded is considered a sign of defensiveness or aloofness. Your posture should show you relaxed yet alert.
3. *Make eye contact, but not too much.* Interviewers don't like being stared at any more than you do.
4. *Anticipate the questions you'll be asked.* Be prepared to tell the interviewer why you're looking for work, what your strengths and weaknesses are, what benefits you can bring to the company. Expect the unexpected. As part of your preparation for your interview, you may want to go through a trial run the night before with your spouse or a friend. (Several books listed at the end of this chapter have in-depth discussions of how to prepare for and conduct an interview.)
5. *Remain calm.* If a question catches you off guard, do your best. And by all means, don't dwell on a mistake if you flub an answer. Concentrate on the moment, not on the past.
6. *If you don't know something, admit it.* An interviewer can see through a bluff immediately. It's far better to say, "I don't know." You may gain the respect of the interviewer for your honesty.
7. *Be enthusiastic.* Remember, your prospective employer wants enthusiastic employees. If you are genuinely interested in the job, act like you *want* to work there.

If you're diligently preparing your résumé, answering want ads, considering employment agencies, building up a network of contacts, and learning how to be interviewed, you are well on your way to getting through your employment crisis in the best shape possible. But you need to take just one more step.

PLAN FINANCIALLY

In chapters 6 and 8, I will be discussing ways of conserving money and identifying hidden sources of income and capital. However, if you know or even think you may lose your job, the time to start saving funds is now. Do not wait months or even weeks from now to locate and conserve your money sources. In fact, you should start to read chapters 6 and 8 *now*.

If you have already lost your job, these measures of money conservation become more urgent. You may be living on savings or unemployment compensation. That helps, but those resources will eventually expire. Therefore, *start planning financially today*.

Maybe you think that if you diligently follow the first three steps— pray, consider your options, and get ready—you will get a job next month or next week. Thus financial planning is a lower priority with you. You may indeed locate the job soon. But sometimes even the best-planned, most carefully executed, diligent job searches drag on for months and even years.

You should be optimistic, of course. (Continued optimism is important during a time of job crisis.) But don't bank (pun intended) on being rehired tomorrow. Plan your financial strategies on the assumption that you're in this for the long haul. You won't lose anything if you do. Even if you get hired tomorrow, you'll have learned some valuable lessons in financial planning.

I highly commend the above four steps of preparation for unemployment. Follow them, and you're well on your way to licking the crisis of impending unemployment. Ignore them, and you do so at your own risk.

The following books all contain information on writing résumés and cover letters. Those followed by (I) also discuss the job interview.

Bolles, Richard N. *What Color Is Your Parachute?* Berkeley, Calif.: Ten Speed, 1990. Updated annually. (I)

Frähm, David J., and Paula Rinehart. *The Great Niche Hunt.* Colorado Springs: NavPress, 1991.

Half, Robert. *How to Get a Better Job in This Crazy World.* New York: Crown, 1990. (I)

Krannich, Ronald L. *Re-Careering in Turbulent Times.* Manassas, Va.: Impact, 1983. (I)

Michelozzi, Betty Neville. *Coming Alive from Nine to Five*, 3d edition. Mountain View, Calif.: Mayfield, 1988. (I)

Peskin, Dean B. *Sacked.* New York: Amacon, 1979. (I)

Snelling, Robert O., Sr. *The Right Job.* New York: Penguin, 1987. (I)

5
Time for a Change?

*E*d Mueller gazed absentmindedly out the window of his office at Bailey and Associates. His eyes hardly saw the morning light shimmer on the reflecting pond below. The late-arriving drivers were searching for the remaining spots in the parking lot of the large office complex, but Ed did not notice. He was absorbed in his thoughts.

He had already checked his calendar and knew that his first meeting was at 9:30 with the creative department; there they would discuss fine-tuning the upcoming advertising campaign for the Weaver's Pretzel account. This would be a typically trying meeting. Ever since Bailey had hired a new art director, *all* the meetings with the creative staff were trying. The rest of the morning would be spent on the phone, persuading prospective clients to sign on with Bailey. Ed had never liked making phone calls. Over the past few months, as he gradually lost his enthusiasm for promoting the company, these calls became sheer torture.

The rest of the day would be trying too. The calendar read "lunch at Sharkey's—Bill Nelson." Bill owned Klein's Department Store, and Klein's was a long-standing account that Ed had brought to Bailey some ten years earlier. Bill had always been easy to work with, but he had recently expressed some disappointment with the way Bailey had been handling their account. Ed would have to try to straighten things out.

The afternoon would bring a meeting with Jim, the account supervisor. Ed knew that Jim would be wondering why the Midwest Bottling account had been lost. Jim never seemed to quite believe that some things were simply beyond Ed's control. He would spend the remainder of the day checking with the production department to make sure it was meeting its deadlines on his accounts and touching base with a couple clients on upcoming campaigns.

Yes, Ed had a full day ahead of him—and he dreaded every minute of it. Just like he had dreaded every minute of yesterday and the day before that.

As Ed sat at his desk that morning, he thought about how happy he had been when he had first come to Bailey fresh out of college fifteen years earlier. After advancing through several positions, he had become an account executive ten years ago. His account supervisor marveled at Ed's enthusiasm and even considered grooming Ed to replace him when he retired. However, as time went on, Ed began to find the pressure of balancing the needs of his clients against the ideas of the creative staff and the limitations of the production department more than he could handle. His long-standing aversion to meeting people began to surface. Increasingly he found it difficult to bring new business into the agency. Ed eventually grew to hate every aspect of his job.

And so, as Ed gazed at the shimmering glass and steel of the Lintell Building beyond the reflecting pond, he reached a conclusion. He would start looking for another job. He didn't know exactly what he wanted to do. But he knew two things. He didn't want to work for Bailey and Associates any longer. And he didn't want to be an advertising account executive.

Had Ed Mueller not been so absorbed in his own problems that morning, he might have noticed the windows on the top floor of the Lintell Building. That's where the executive suites of the Lintell Corporation, a large communications firm, were located. Wes Barker, vice president of marketing, sat behind his desk in one of those suites, facing pressures of his own.

Wes was already on his fifth cup of coffee. He needed it to keep awake. The night before he had stayed up till midnight working on a report due on the president's desk the next morning. With a full day of work ahead of him, Wes had left his new four-bedroom home in Sandalwood at six o'clock for the half hour drive to his office.

It had been like this for quite some time. Sixteen-hour days and eighty-hour weeks were not at all unusual for Wes. Weekends were seldom free for the family. But this is what Lintell expected of its executives. And Wes was the model executive. Having come to Lintell with his MBA in marketing eighteen years earlier, he was on the corporate "fast track." The current president of Lintell was just a few years short of retirement. Wes was one of the leading candidates to replace him.

But Wes was miserable. He had almost no time to spend with his wife, and he felt he hardly knew his children any more. Years ago he had been active in his church, teaching Sunday school and even serving a term on the board of deacons. But all this had fallen by the wayside as his corporate responsibilities consumed more and more of his time. His schedule was even beginning to affect his health. He had abandoned his exercise program for lack of time, and his diet pretty much consisted of cup after cup of coffee with a quick bite to eat grabbed on the run.

Although that morning Wes was far too busy to take a moment to reflect, he too knew that something had to change. And he knew that he had to choose between moving up the Lintell corporate ladder and the other things he valued.

At that very moment, Sandy McIlvane was going through a similar struggle in Lintell's payroll department. After graduating from high school, Sandy had worked as a payroll clerk for another firm for three years and had come to Lintell ten years ago. She really enjoyed the atmosphere in Lintell's payroll department. There was only one problem. Sandy felt unfulfilled.

Sandy was very good at listening to other people and helping them solve their problems. Having been through a painful divorce five years earlier, she had a special empathy for women going through marital crises.

When she told her pastor of her desire to help such women, he suggested she take a couple counseling courses at the local community college. These courses served to further whet her appetite. She now faced a decision. Should she leave Lintell and go to school full time to get her counseling degree? Or should she stick it out as a payroll clerk and perhaps lose her chance to do what she really wanted to do? Her decision had major implications for her time and budget as a single mom with two preteen children to support.

Sandy pondered her decision for several weeks. But as the time went on, she became convinced that she had to do what she really wanted to do. As she took her coffee break that morning, she prayed once again for guidance. That afternoon she made up her mind. She would hand in her resignation and go to school full time.

---

*O**ur job dissatisfaction may grow gradually. But sooner or later most people will experience a career crisis.***

It goes by various names: *job dissatisfaction, burnout, midlife crisis.* Whatever we call it, it's a time when we reexamine where we are going in our career. We don't simply speculate on what it might be like to do something different. We do more than daydream about leaving the rat race and opening an inn along the New England coast. Rather, we go through a soul-searching, gut-wrenching questioning of the wisdom of continuing on the path we have been traveling our whole adult life.

The job dissatisfaction may be triggered by a crisis in our personal life, such as a divorce, or in our professional life, such as an unexpected demotion (or promotion). Or our dissatisfaction may grow gradually, almost imperceptibly, over a long period of time. But sooner or later, most people in the work force experience a career crisis.

In fact, many will experience several in their lifetime. It is estimated that the average worker will change jobs eight times during his or her adult life. Some of these changes will be from one company to another within the same industry. They may be made simply out of a desire to move ahead or to relocate in a different part of the country. Others, however, will involve a whole new career. A person may leave teaching college math to become a nurse. He may leave the newspaper business to become a lawyer. He may even resign as the president of a textile manufacturer to plant a vineyard.[1]

Gone are the days of retiring with a gold watch after forty-five years of faithful service to one company. Few people still follow this course. The reasons for change vary, but many will change some of their jobs due to job dissatisfaction for one reason or another.

Some career crises are best solved by finding a new profession. When a person is miscast in his or her current profession, a new career may be the only viable solution. Sometimes, however, working in one's chosen field for another company is the answer. Sometimes moving into a job in another department resolves the problem. Occasionally the crisis may be averted simply by changing certain facets of one's current job. Those going through career crises must not only identify the cause but must be guided to the proper solution as well.

CAUSES OF CAREER CRISES

Before we consider how to resolve career crises, let's identify the causes. People experience career crises for one or more of seven major reasons:

- They are miscast in their career.
- They are overworked or underworked.
- They are unhappy with their work environment.
- Their work is inconsistent with their values and ideals.
- Their work does not provide adequate compensation.
- Their work does not allow them to use all their skills and training.
- Their work does not provide a sense of personal fulfillment.

Let's now examine each of these causes in turn.

The Wrong Career

Few people thoroughly assess their strengths and weaknesses before choosing a career. Much more often they get into their first career because they're following in their father's footsteps (or intentionally avoiding his footsteps), they're trying to satisfy their parents' wishes, they took the advice of someone they admired, their college major prepared them for it, or they simply found a job open in the field when it was time to go out to work. Put simply, *they fall into their career.*

Providentially, some people happen upon a career that perfectly suits their talents and inclinations. Too many, however, are like Ed Mueller. A few of their talents match the skills needed in the job. But they also lack the talents or inclinations required for other important aspects of their job. They may be able to hide these inadequacies for a time. Eventually they surface. When they do, job dissatisfaction soon follows.

Ed Mueller came to his job with certain definite strengths. He had a good sense for what his clients were looking for in their advertising campaigns. He knew how to translate this for the creative staff. He also was good at paying attention to detail. This allowed him to catch potential snafus in the production process of an ad campaign. But Ed was not a "people person." Not only was he very uncomfortable meeting new people, but he was not adept at handling conflicts with his coworkers. Account executives, however, need strong people skills. For a while, Ed's enthusiasm for his work masked his weakness. When his enthusiasm wore thin over time, he grew to hate his job.

Some careers require a wide variety of extremely diverse talents. School administration is a case in point. A principal is expected to be a good public speaker, a financial whiz, a counselor, a wise disciplinarian, a public relations expert, a youth worker, a warm, affable individual, and a top-notch administrator. Few principals are gifted in all these areas. A man or woman with strong counseling skills may be a feeble public speaker. An adept administrator may be an abrasive person, with little ability or desire to extend himself to others. Someone gifted in community relations may be totally unable to relate to young people. It is not at all surprising that principals are prone to burnout. Many of them may be thoroughly miscast in their roles.

But miscasting frequently occurs in careers that don't require nearly the range of diverse skills needed by school principals. People who have no patience with details become accountants. There are salesmen who dread making cold calls. And social butterflies wind up as copywriters, spending most of their time in their cubicles, churning out words. Sooner or later, such people will become extremely frustrated in their jobs. In extreme cases, they may become totally unable to function.

Overwork and Underwork

Men and women find themselves overworked for a variety of reasons. Some, like Wes Barker, work for a company that expects its employees (or at least its executives) to be "married" to their jobs. Others may simply lack the requisite speed for a particular task that takes up a significant share of their daily routine. For instance, a secretary who can't type more than forty words per minute will fall behind much more often than one with the same work load who can type one hundred words per minute.

When job dissatisfaction is due to overwork, finding out its cause is essential. A secretary may be falling behind because she can't type adequately. In this case, the solution is for her either to get further training or to find a job that doesn't require typing skills. On the other hand, she may be working in an office that really needs two secretaries (or perhaps an additional part-time person). The solution to her problem is not for her to find another career. She may indeed be the "ideal" secretary. She needs to convince her boss that the workload requires an additional person.

Slow and Too Easy

When it comes to job dissatisfaction, having too little work can be as frustrating as having too much. Annette Fox loved what she was doing, but she was underworked; eventually job dissatisfaction set in.

Annette was employed as a copywriter in the public relations department of a large nonprofit organization. Her boss had held Annette's job before he was promoted to department manager. Although he was an extremely good writer, he was also very slow, often agonizing at length over each sentence. Annette was capable of producing quality work in a fraction of the time. Her boss didn't realize this, and he assigned her only the amount of work he could have handled in an eight-hour day. Annette soon realized that if she didn't say something, she would be sitting in her office days on end without any work.

Eventually, Annette spoke to her boss. However, he was unresponsive, muttering, "Well, I really don't have any more work at this time. We'll see if something comes up later." It rarely did.

Over time, Annette became bored and then frustrated. Eventually she found a job with another organization.

The underworked person may become dissatisfied with his job a bit more slowly. And he may never experience the burnout the overworked executive feels. But underwork is still a problem, and it can lead to boredom and extreme frustration.

As with overwork, the solutions to underwork are varied, and finding the proper one will require determining the cause. The big difference is that a person who is underworked is never in this situation because he lacks the skills necessary to adequately perform his job. If anything, his skills are far beyond what he needs for his assigned tasks. To avoid boredom, he may need a heavier workload or a promotion to a position of greater responsibility. Occasionally, he may be unable to fully utilize his skills in the career he has chosen. If so, a career switch may be in order.

The Work Environment

Fran Martin had worked in the underwriting department of Union Mutual Casualty for nearly twenty years. Starting out as a file clerk, she had worked her way up to assistant supervisor of the Midwest district. Over the

From Chicago to Philadelphia to Chaos

Dissatisfaction with the work environment includes the physical surroundings. The physical environment extends far beyond the walls of the workplace itself. A person may become extremely frustrated by an hour-long commute to work through heavy traffic. He may even become depressed by having to live in a certain part of the country.

When I was four years old, my dad was transferred by his company from Chicago to Philadelphia. Dad was chief accountant with an insurance company, and now he and my mom were far away from their bothers and sisters. The adjustment was very difficult; in fact, Dad and Mom never fully adjusted.

As a result, within three years he found a job with another insurance company, and we moved back to the Chicago area. Indeed, we bought a house in the same suburb we had lived in before. Dad no longer was chief accountant; but he gladly accepted the demotion. Though the move back cost us money, my dad knew his frustration with the new physical environment was not worth it.

He remained in Chicago, near my aunts and uncles, for the rest of his working years. Dad was satisfied with his job because, for him, there was no place like home. The physical environment gave him true job satisfaction.

years, she had seen most of her coworkers come and go. And that's where her problem lay. When she started at Union Mutual, she had immediately developed a rapport with many of the people in the office. But her best friends had either retired or left. She found it difficult to warm up to the young men and women who had been hired recently. Most of them were younger than her children, and their interests and values were different from hers.

Moreover, her immediate supervisor, who had recently been hired from another company, was an uncommunicative, rather surly fellow. Although Fran was close friends with the department manager, he was going to retire in a couple years, and she had no idea who would replace him. For years, Fran had looked forward to going to work. Recently it had become a burden.

Fran's problem was the *people environment* in her workplace. The *physical environment* can also cause frustration. People may react very differently to the same physical surroundings. One person may find a din-gy, dirty factory terribly oppressive. The fellow working next to him may hardly notice. An office without windows or adequate ventilation may create claustrophobia in one worker. His coworker may find the same conditions ideal for work. Some people are ideally suited for sitting at a desk eight hours a day, five days a week, fifty weeks of the year. Others are driven crazy by this regimen.

Frustration with one's work environment can be alleviated in many different ways. If the problem is the physical environment, the solution is rather simple. Either adjust or find another job. If career dissatisfaction is involved as well, the proper move may be to change careers as well as jobs. Interpersonal dynamics are more complex. We may need to be more accepting of those with whom we work. Perhaps we need to patch up differences. Perhaps the boss really is a tyrant. Perhaps we are an artistic type among an office full of conventional people. The proper solution will depend on an accurate assessment of the problem, and that isn't always easy.

Inconsistency with Values and Ideals

When Liz Jarman was hired as a nurse at Midtown General Hospital, she hadn't thought much about abortion. Not long afterward, her pastor gave a series of sermons on the issue. The series had a profound impact on her. After talking over the issue with her friends at church, she became ardently pro-life. She now faced a dilemma. Doctors at Midtown General performed abortions. Because she worked in the oncology unit, she knew she would never personally have to participate in an abortion procedure. Still, she didn't believe that she could, in good conscience, remain part of an organization that permitted such operations. As a result, she put in her application at nearby St. Mary's. A few weeks later, St. Mary's called about an opening in their oncology unit. Liz handed in her resignation the same day, grateful that she was no longer part of the Midtown General team.

Many employees never face the dilemma of being confronted in their workplace by a practice they find morally offensive. Many others do. Like Liz, they may be on the staff of a hospital where abortions are practiced. They may work for a corporation that manufactures unsafe products or wantonly pollutes the environment. They may be specifically asked to falsify records or take part in dishonest business dealings.

Placed in this situation, they have to decide on a course of action. Do they go along with the practice, somehow rationalizing their involvement? Do they protest, hoping they can influence their employer to change things? Or do they begin to look for another job? Each case must be handled individually. And each person involved must ultimately answer these questions for himself. But as long as sin is in this world, workers will encounter these dilemmas. Christian employees in particular must be aware of the practices of their employers, and they must live with a free conscience before God—even if this means finding another job.

Inadequate Compensation

Dave Doty had worked for more than twenty years in the data processing department of Harrison Laboratories. He had an impeccable work record. Rarely absent and never tardy, he had always received excellent evaluations from his superiors. Dave had not advanced and his salary had begun to lag behind that of his coworkers. By comparing notes with data processors in other firms in town, he knew that he was grossly underpaid.

Dave wasn't greedy. He and his family were content to live modestly. Still, the fact that he was not being paid what he was worth began to rankle him. For the most part, Dave had been happy at Harrison Labs. But as his anger over his inadequate salary grew, little annoyances began to be blown out of proportion. Because he was never one to press an issue with his superiors, complaining about his salary was out of the question. He did the only thing he felt he could do. He began looking for another job. When he was offered one at a higher salary in the data processing department of a large insurance company, he left.

Inadequate compensation takes many forms; the salary issue is simply the most obvious. Lack of adequate fringe benefits, lack of praise or recognition, failure to receive a deserved promotion, and lack of prestige all contribute to job frustration. Some of these factors, being less concrete, are all the more insidious as a result. A person who has not received an adequate raise may be able to easily identify this as his source of frustration. That same person may be smarting because he has not received the praise he deserves or because his job lacks prestige. He may not even recognize that this is why he's dissatisfied.

Unused Skills and Training

Linda Schubert was an art major in college and had taken graduate courses in commercial art as well. For seven years she had worked in the art department of Bucknell and Brister, a large advertising firm. Bucknell had unusual job stability, particularly in its art department. As a result, Linda had never advanced beyond her entry-level position. While she was able to use certain of her artistic talents on the projects to which she was assigned, she had almost no input in the design of new advertising copy. She felt that most of her training was going to waste. As a result, when she was offered a job with an interior decorating company, she jumped at the opportunity, despite having to take a substantial cut in pay.

Linda typifies another source of job dissatisfaction—unused or under-utilized skills and training. One example of this is someone with a doctor-ate in English working on a factory assembly line. Most cases aren't so extreme. More typically, people find themselves in a position similar to Linda's—using some of their skills but not all of them. A skilled pianist, for example, may be forced to teach elementary school music to make ends meet. Or a gifted creative writer may have become locked into a job writing technical manuals. No matter what the skill, or the extent it is under-utilized, someone whose job does not properly use his skills or training is likely to become extremely frustrated.

Lack of Personal Fulfillment

A person may have a job commensurate with his skills and training. He may be kept busy without being overworked. He may find his work environment quite pleasant. He may be adequately compensated. He may have no conflict with the values of his employer. Yet, he may still be un-happy, for he may still find his job to be utterly unfulfilling.

Sandy McIlvane provides a good example. Although relatively happy with her work environment, Sandy wanted to do more with her life than work in the payroll department of the Lintell Company. And so she left to go back to school.

It's impossible to fully understand why one person will find himself perfectly suited to a situation and another equally gifted person will re-main unfulfilled. But it happens all the time. One man thrives on moving up the corporate ladder. Another equally successful executive is left feel-ing empty. One woman finds teaching fulfilling. Her colleague doubts that he's having a lasting impact on the students that pass through his classes year after year. One fellow retires from his job as a claims adjuster, quite content with what he has done. His coworker wishes he could do it all over again.

Nor do we always find people fulfilled in the ways we would antici-pate. College professors have resigned their prestigious and well-compen-sated positions as department chairmen and have contentedly lived out their lives working in a factory. Burned-out pastors have found fulfillment as accountants in insurance companies. And doctors have become brick-layers.

Of the seven causes of job dissatisfaction, lack of personal fulfill-ment is clearly the most nebulous. Not surprisingly, then, it's also the har-dest to identify and the most difficult to overcome. Still, it must be recognized. And the person who is suffering a career crisis because of it must try to find a solution.

SOLUTIONS TO A JOB CRISIS

If you're suffering from job dissatisfaction for one of these seven reasons, what are your options? One of the following may offer you the right
solution.

Do Nothing

If you're near retirement, this may be your best option. However, too
many people who still have many years of productive work ahead of them
wind up doing nothing. They take refuge in their hobbies, their families,
their weekends, and in some cases in alcohol or other addictive behavior.
Work becomes more and more of a burden. Some of these people survive
like this for years. Others become so indifferent to their jobs that they get
demoted or fired. The "solution" becomes worse than the problem.

Change Careers

Perhaps you're miscast in your career. The obvious solution is for
you to find a new career. However, finding a new career often means a
period of retraining. This may require schooling, which can be expensive
and disruptive to family life. At the very least, it means identifying talents
and abilities that can be transferred to another occupation. (And it may
not be easy to convince a prospective employer that such talents and abilities are transferable.) So, you'll probably want to consider a new career at
this point only if you're sure you're "a square peg in a round hole."

How can you know this? The obvious cases are easy to identify. A
salesman who, after five years, still breaks out into a cold sweat every time
he has to make a call, or who can't bring himself to ask someone to buy
his product, is in the wrong line of work. So is the insurance underwriter
who gazes out of the office window every day wishing he could be a forest
ranger or a fishing guide. Unfortunately, most cases aren't so straightforward.

One way to find out is to take one (or several) of a number of available tests. These tests are designed to identify your personality type, your
interests, your talents, and the like. Most career counseling centers admin-
ister them. Often they form part of talent assessment seminars. Or you
may test yourself. Many books on vocational planning contain these tests.
(Several books that do are listed at the end of this chapter.)

If you're miscast in your job, you have several alternatives. You may
want to go back to school to receive training for another career. You may
be able to convince a potential employer that your skills are transferable
to a different line of work. You may even find that your present employer is
willing to retrain you or transfer you to a job more suitable to your talents

and personality. Or you may consider self-employment. Whichever alternative you take, however, make sure you really are getting into something more suitable. Otherwise your move to a new career is merely a leap "out of the frying pan and into the fire."

Change Companies

You may have to change companies if you are miscast in your present job. But this may also be the best course of action if your job dissatisfaction is a result of your work environment, a lack of adequate compensation, overwork or underwork, or an employer engaged in practices inconsistent with your values.

A job switch costs time and ... can be exhausting. You may even lose certain benefits. ... But sometimes leaving one employer for another is the right thing to do.

Leaving one employer for another should never be taken lightly. A job search costs time—and sometimes considerable money as well. It can be exhausting. You may even lose certain benefits (such as pension benefits). But sometimes leaving one employer for another is the right thing to do.

Nurse Jarman provides a perfect example. Had she continued at Midtown General, she would have had to compromise her beliefs concerning abortion. Her only viable option was to find another job.

The issue isn't always so clear-cut. If your work environment is the problem, you can often do something about it. Perhaps you work in a dingy office without ventilation. But maybe your employer will be receptive to your suggestions for improvement.

Lack of adequate compensation is another case in point. If the issue is something as straightforward as not getting paid enough, you may be able to work this through with your boss. It's certainly worth a try—particularly if you don't already have something else lined up. However, if you find yourself in a dead-end job without any possibility of advancement and it's important for you to advance in your career, finding another job may be the only alternative.

If you're overworked or underworked, you might try getting your job description changed. You may be surprised at how receptive your employer is. (He or she may have been thinking along the same lines.) If it turns out that you run up against a brick wall, *that* may be your sign to start looking elsewhere.

Change Jobs Within a Company

Seeking a new job within your present company is a strategy I've already mentioned as an alternative to changing careers or employers. Most companies want their workers to be happy. They also want to keep their good employees. If your job isn't challenging enough or requires skills you don't possess, your employer may be only too happy to accommodate your request for a change—particularly if you demonstrate that it's to his advantage as well.

Dolores Stevens had been employed as a copywriter for a Christian publishing company for more than fifteen years when she was promoted to the position of manager of the periodicals department. Although an excellent writer, Delores was quite incapable of running a department. She had no idea how to communicate instructions to her subordinates. Deadlines came and went before she made assignments. And she had no idea how to keep the simplest project flowing smoothly. Although they liked her, the staff writers knew she was a terrible boss. The vice president who had recommended her for the position privately admitted his blunder but was afraid to say anything to her for fear of hurting her feelings. And Dolores herself became miserable, as she saw the disarray she was creating.

This went on for more than two years. Finally, when the job of assistant book editor opened up, Dolores applied. Even though it was technically a step down, Dolores knew she would be much happier. The company vice president was elated at this solution to his problem. And the members of the periodicals department breathed a collective sigh of relief.

Change Your Job Description

You may find that you enjoy your job as a whole but that there's a specific aspect you simply hate. You may be able to alleviate this by eliminating this aspect from your job. Talk to your fellow workers. You may be able to trade off. Talk to your bosses. They may have some suggestions. Remember, if you're a good employee, most employers will do anything within reason to keep you happy and keep you working for them. It's certainly worth a try and a whole lot easier than finding another job.

Change Yourself

Perhaps you're having a personality problem with one of your co-workers or your boss. It may have reached the point where you're miserable as a result. Maybe it's totally the other person's fault. But this isn't likely. Personality conflicts are usually a two-way street. You may not be able to change the other person, but you can change the way you relate to that person.

Or perhaps you hate working in an office without a window or being forced to drive half an hour through rush hour traffic. You can always decide to look for another job. But remember, no job is perfect. Maybe you should try adjusting to your situation.

Or perhaps it's that one task that seems incredibly boring. Well, there are always going to be things in life that are boring. Brushing your teeth is incredibly boring. But you do it every day. If you like most of your job, maybe it's worth putting up with its boring aspects and making the best of them.

So, if you're frustrated with your job, you have several options. You can find a new career, change jobs, find a new position within your present company, change your job description, change yourself, or do nothing. The choice is yours. But whatever you do, remember, you're making an important decision. Think it through thoroughly beforehand. Get feedback from people you trust. And above all, pray about it.

The following books contain personality tests or talent-assessment exercises to aid you in your career search:

Bolles, Richard N. *What Color Is Your Parachute?* Berkeley, Calif.: Ten Speed, 1990.

Bradley, John, and Jay Carty. *Unlocking Your Sixth Suitcase.* Colorado Springs: NavPress, 1991.

Frähm, David J., and Paula Rinehart. *The Great Niche Hunt.* Colorado Springs: NavPress, 1991.

Haldane, Bernard. *Career Satisfaction and Success.* New York: Amacon, 1981.

Michelozzi, Betty Neville. *Coming Alive from Nine to Five,* 3d edition. Mountain View, Calif.: Mayfield, 1988.

Voges, Ken and Ron Braund. *Understanding How Others Misunderstand You Workbook.* Chicago: Moody, 1991.

6
Scaling Down: Becoming a One-Income Family in a Two-Income World

When Mark and Janice Ross had their first baby, Janice took a short leave of absence from her job with an accounting firm. Six weeks after little Paul was born she was back to work. Mark and she hated the hassle of driving Paul to and from the baby-sitter every day, and she was especially disturbed by Paul's frequent colds and bouts with the flu, a result of his constant exposure to other young children. Moreover, she longed for more time with Paul than the few tired hours she had in the evening. But she didn't see how she could afford to quit work. Mark's job as a clerk in an appliance store was secure, but it didn't pay very well. They needed her salary to pay the mortgage on the home they had just purchased.

Two years later Janice was pregnant again. Realizing that a second child would mean greater baby-sitting expense and would create additional juggling of schedules, Mark and Janice decided to take stock. If Mark stayed home, the financial burden would not be quite so great. His salary was only about two-thirds of hers. Yes, Janice could continue to work, but she knew that kissing *two* children goodbye each morning would simply increase her loathing for her job. Janice really wanted to be the one to nurture the children during the day.

Paul soon had a little sister, Amy, and their mother had a question: Should I work at all? Janice considered cutting back to part-time. This would allow her to spend more hours with the children without severe loss of income. But the hassle of running Paul and Amy to the baby-sitter would remain, as would their constant exposure to all sorts of childhood ailments.

She thought about working at home; she could operate an independent accounting service. This would eliminate the baby-sitter problem. However, building up a clientele would take time and energy. Mark wasn't sure they could survive the time before the income would start flowing. Janice questioned whether she would have the energy to devote to caring for two small children *and* finding clients for her business.

Janice regarded the third alternative—staying home and not working —as impossible. At the very least, it would require selling their house, finding a much more modest place to live, and scaling back their lifestyle almost beyond what they could imagine.

Mark and Janice's predicament is typical of many couples in today's society. Having become accustomed to a lifestyle that requires two incomes, they don't see how they can possibly get by on one. At the same time, they find the trade-off—leaving their children in day care or with a baby-sitter—to be intolerable. For many couples, having one parent at home to nurture the children is a benefit worth almost any sacrifice.

This predicament extends beyond couples with young children. Sometimes a spouse suffers from job burnout and needs time away from the work force. A different spouse may long to do volunteer work or go back to school. And some would simply like to have time to enjoy being at home. In each of these cases, quitting a job means scaling back one's lifestyle, finding another way of generating income, or sometimes doing both.

Single parents and unmarried individuals face a similar situation. If they want to leave the paycheck security the work force provides, they may find alternate ways of making money, but they still must adjust their lifestyle to live with less. They too need to know how this can be done.

Subsequent chapters will discuss ways to earn money at home (see especially chapters 8 and 13). At present, we will consider how to scale back on one's lifestyle and become a successful one-income family in a two-income world.

We should see money as a gift, a blessing from God to be held lightly. ...We should never be trapped by the lure of the affluent lifestyle.

The apostle Paul says, "Godliness with contentment is great gain. For we brought nothing into the world, and we can take nothing out of it. But if we have food and clothing, we will be content with that. People who want to get rich fall into temptation and a trap and into many foolish and harmful desires that plunge men into ruin and destruction. For the love of money is a root of all kinds of evil" (1 Timothy 6:6-10).

Every Christian should know this passage and internalize it. Money itself is not evil. The *love* of money is at the root of much evil. The Christian should see money as a gift, a blessing from God to be held lightly. So long as he has what he truly needs—food to keep him from hunger, clothing to keep him warm, shelter to protect him from the elements—he should be content.

The Christian should never be trapped by the lure of the affluent, acquisitive lifestyle. This does not mean that Christians ought never to be rich. Material riches are a sign of God's blessing. (See, for example, Genesis 26:12-13; Deuteronomy 28:1-14; Psalm 107:37-38.) When God blesses us in this way, we can certainly praise and thank Him for what He has done. But the Christian also must recognize that material possessions are not all-important. At times his obedience to God may require that he adopt a simpler lifestyle than his unbelieving neighbor. The Christian may find that rearing and educating his children, doing volunteer work for the kingdom, and being actively involved in his church take precedence over earning as much money as possible.

Although we cannot lay down hard and fast rules for every believer, each Christian must seriously examine his motivation for what he is doing and order his priorities according to the principle his Lord laid down: "Seek first [God's] kingdom and his righteousness" (Matthew 6:33). Sometimes this motivation means you may want—and be able to live with—fewer possessions.

"But we need two incomes to make ends meet!" you may say. Yes, in some cases a family truly needs two full-time incomes, but such instances are rare. I can make that claim with confidence for three reasons. First, the second income rarely adds all that much to a couple's true overall income. Second, the second income typically is spent on nonessentials. Third, almost all two-income families are in a position to simplify their living standards in many areas and still have the essentials for living spoken of by Paul. Let's look at each of these reasons in turn.

THE SECOND-INCOME FALLACY

The second-income fallacy is the belief that a second full-time income doubles or nearly doubles a family's real income. To begin with, in most families, the second income is considerably smaller than the first. For instance, the husband may be making $25,000 a year, the wife $16,000. I am assuming that the person making the lesser income is the one who will be quitting his or her job. (Mark and Janice, then, are the exception to the rule. Though Mark earns less, he will continue to work; Janet's larger income, however, may require that she find at least some part-time income.) When the income differential is sizeable, cutting back to one income may reduce a family's gross income by as little as a third.

But let's take a case in which a husband and wife with two children are each earning 50 percent of the family's gross income. Jeff and Lynn Sathers are making $20,000 each for a combined income of $40,000. If one of them were to quit work, their gross income would be cut in half. But the Sathers would soon find that the money they had each month on which to live would have decreased far less.

First, taxes would take a smaller bite out of the remaining salary. As of 1990, a family of four that does not itemize its deductions pays no federal tax on its first $13,650 in income. If that family's adjusted gross income were $40,000, it would pay $3,956 in taxes, leaving them $36,044. That same family with an adjusted gross income of $20,000 would pay $956, leaving $19,044. This alone brings the income differential down to $17,000.[2] Subtract from this figure the approximately $1,500 less that will be paid into Social Security and the differential now stands at $15,500.

State and local income taxes are impossible to calculate with any accuracy because they vary so much from location to location. Given that most state income taxes are progressive (i.e., they increase in percentage as income increases), a good ballpark figure for the differential once they are factored in would be $15,000.

Now, $15,000 is still a big difference. But this is just the start. When husband and wife both work outside the home, they both need transportation. Public transportation, where available, is expensive. A second car means additional gas and oil, maintenance, insurance, and very likely monthly payments on a loan. With little imagination we can see that figure shrinking to $14,000, maybe even less. Add to this expenses for dress clothes and at least some lunches eaten at a restaurant near work and we're closing in on $13,000.

The biggest crunch, though, comes for families with small children. The Sathers have two children, one who is too young for school. Child care expenses vary from one part of the country to another, but an average figure for full-time care is $4,000 per year. The differential for the Sathers is now down to $9,000.

So, if the Sathers needed child care, the true differential when only one parent works is $9,000. (For those without child care, the differential is $13,000.) And remember, in this family, the husband and wife's salary are equal. If the husband earned $25,000 a year and his wife $15,000, and the wife quit her job, the actual differential would be less—only $5,650 when child care is included.[3] All of a sudden working outside the home doesn't seem to be such a bargain.

But, you say, $13,000 is still a lot of money, although considerably less than the $20,000 with which we started. And $5,650, although perhaps hardly worth the hassle of going out to work every day, is still better than nothing. It may even be the difference between making and not making ends meet.

True, yet this is only the first reason for my claim that two incomes aren't necessary to make ends meet. Let's consider the next two.

WEEDING OUT THE NONESSENTIALS

Most budgets include nonessential expenses. Consider again Jeff and Lynn Sather. When their gross income is reduced by $20,000 a year, they will find that they have between $9,000 and $13,000 less to spend each year, depending on whether or not they have child care expenses. But let's see how they're spending their money.

Much of their—and our—spending is for discretionary purchases. VCRs, camcorders, new television sets, expensive vacations, and eating at fancy restaurants are not required for satisfying our basic needs. Often we spend at our discretion, or choice, instead of need. Although spending money on such items is not wrong, the goods are not necessary for our contentment.

Obviously, families vary widely in how much they spend on discretionary purchases. While many families spend far more (and a few spend considerably less), I would estimate that if the Sathers are typical, they spend about $4,000 a year in this way.

I wouldn't expect Jeff and Lynn to eliminate all discretionary purchases. But if one wage earner is going to stay home, the Sathers should cut back to $1,000, at least until they know they can afford more. This will still permit a modest but nice family vacation and an occasional meal at a restaurant. It will also mean they have saved an additional $3,000. Their income differential is now down to somewhere between $6,000 and $10,000.

Of course, they still need money for such necessities as food and clothing. In chapter 8 I will discuss ways of economizing in these areas in much more detail. At present, consider these money-saving strategies: (1) clipping coupons, (2) stocking up on sale items, (3) resisting impulse purchases at the grocery store, (4) carefully planning trips to the store to conserve gas, (5) avoiding snack foods between meals, (6) and buying clothes for the family at garage sales and thrift shops. My personal experience has shown me that a family can save as much as $2,000 per year in these ways.

The Sathers have now lowered the differential to between $4,000 and $8,000 per year. (For a family of four with child care expenses and in which the primary wage earner is making $25,000 of the $40,000 total, that differential has now been eliminated entirely.)

The Sathers can also save on their housing costs, which along with food and clothing form the three basic material necessities of life.

L ocation should be a low priority in choosing a house. Yet location is often the greatest single factor affecting a house's price, and most buyers spend too much seeking location.

Many two-income families are saddled with a mortgage close to the maximum they can get from the bank based on both incomes. A couple with combined earnings of $40,000 per year will be able to get a mortgage with monthly payments (including taxes and insurance) in the neighborhood of $930. In most parts of the country, $930 per month will purchase a pretty fancy house. (In those cities, such as Los Angeles and New York, where this is not so, combined salaries are likely to be much higher than $40,000 per year. The amount of money the bank lends will also be much greater, as will the monthly mortgage payments.) When a couple tries to determine whether they will be able to get by on one income, they need to ask themselves whether they absolutely need to stay in the house in which they are now living.

There may be exceptions, but most couples, if they were completely honest, would have to answer no to the question "Is living in this house absolutely necessary?" Houses vary in price for a variety of reasons, including their size, condition, and location. Size and condition and possibly age are legitimate considerations in deciding which house to live in. Location should be a very low priority. Yet location is often the greatest single factor affecting the price of a house, and most homebuyers spend more seeking location. In my adopted home town of Lincoln, Nebraska, for example, a house in the Country Club area will cost at least 33 percent more than a comparable house on the north side of town. That same house, located in a small town ten miles away, would be valued at half what it is in the Country Club area. Living in a prestigious part of town is nice, but it should be secondary for the couple in the process of scaling down to one income.

With this in mind, let's go back to the Sathers. Suppose that they are saddled with mortgage payments of $930 per month. If they are willing to sacrifice location, age, and possibly a bit on condition, they can sell their house, use the equity they've built up to put a substantial down payment on a less pretentious dwelling, and still get a very nice house with payments of $580 per month. Thus the Sathers are saving an additional $3,000 per year. We've now got the differential down to between $1,000 and $5,000, and we still haven't taken the final step.

SIMPLIFYING LIFESTYLE

In a sense, what I've said about weeding out the nonessentials is itself part of simplifying one's lifestyle. But there are also ways to dramatically cut our expenditures as we take care of our daily needs.

You can reduce food costs. A well-tended garden can save several hundred dollars a year. If you live in a part of the country where fruit trees flourish, you can add to these savings by planting several and enjoying their fruit. Buying your grain in bulk, grinding it, and baking your own breads and cakes will increase your savings further. Finally, cutting down on red meat and substituting dairy products and grains is not only health-ful but will also drastically reduce your food budget.

You can reduce clothing costs. As mentioned earlier, you can buy clothes second hand. In addition, you will save substantially by sewing your own clothes. Carefully selecting materials that will not readily wear out will also reduce your clothes budget. Blue jeans (*not* of the designer variety) bought from the rack at a discount department store and flannel shirts may not win you a fashion award, but they are comfortable and last a very long time.

You can reduce the cost of shelter. You can conserve substantially on your utility bills by keeping the thermostat turned down in the winter and up in the summer. (Also, a well-placed ceiling or attic fan can help tre-mendously in cutting your costs.) You can get rid of that lawn service and do your own yard. If you've moved from the fashionable part of town, you may not even feel under pressure to keep your grass watered in the sum-mer. You don't have to be a handyman (or woman) to do much of the simple around-the-house maintenance yourself, such as painting, light re-pairs, and the like.

A disclaimer: Not all Christians are called to a simple lifestyle, nor can one enhance his standing with God by adopting such a lifestyle.

At this point I want to issue a disclaimer. I do not want to legislate a series of "dos" and "don'ts" for Christians. For many years before becom-ing a Christian, I was a vegetarian and lived an extremely austere lifestyle. One of the first things I realized when I knew that I had been saved by grace through faith in Jesus Christ was that I was freed from a legalistic attempt to earn my own salvation.

Not all Christians are called to a simple lifestyle, nor can one en-hance his standing with God by adopting such a lifestyle. At the same time, if a Christian couple is seriously committed to cutting back from two incomes to one, they should carefully examine their lifestyle to find ways to simplify.

Just how much you save by taking these (and other) steps will de-pend on your ingenuity and on how simple your lifestyle was to begin with. But it is not unrealistic to think that if you really work at it, you will be able to save between $2,000 and $3,000 per year, possibly even more.

Suppose that the Sathers are able to save $2,000 this way. They're now down to a maximum differential of $3,000. They're almost to the point where they will have a balanced budget, even though they are losing half of their gross income. For a more typical family, where the primary wage earner grosses closer to 60 percent of their total income, that differential has vanished completely by this point. The same holds true if they have been paying for child care out of their second income.

The idea that a family needs two full-time incomes to make ends meet, then, is largely a myth. The typical American family can survive, and can survive quite well, on one full-time paycheck.

WORKING AT HOME

We must also not think that when a husband or wife decides to stay home he or she will contribute nothing to the family's income. It's possible not to generate any income, but certainly not necessary. The stay-at-home partner may work part time outside the home, become a "telecommuter," or even operate a home-based business. Let's consider briefly each alternative.

- *Part-time work.* The stay-at-home spouse may decide to take a part-time job. A mom who wants to spend her days with her children may be able to take an evening or Saturday job to supplement the family's income. A husband or wife going back to school may be able to schedule part-time employment around classes and studies. A person who has quit full-time work to do volunteer activities may still want to continue working for pay fifteen to twenty hours per week.
- *Telecommuting.* A person may be able to work out an arrangement with his employer to work at home. This can be full-time or part-time work. Of course, if it is full-time, it may become nearly as much a burden as full-time out-of-the-home work. But part-time telecommuting may be the ideal solution for people who want to generate income yet have the benefits of staying at home.
- *Home-based business.* Typically a home-based business takes awhile to start generating substantial income. However, if begun sensibly and modestly, it can provide a small amount of income for the family almost from the start. Chapter 13 discusses the pros and cons of home-based businesses and how to go about starting one.

Is it time for your family to become a one-income family? Only you can answer that. You alone know your true needs, your ideals, your goals. But if you and your spouse are both working and you find this arrangement increasingly frustrating, you might consider this alternative. You will be part of a growing number of people who are intentionally scaling down in an upscale world.

7

The Working Woman

The working woman is a common species in the offices and factories of late twentieth-century America. Single women, single
moms, wives who are the primary breadwinners, two-income
families—all these are increasingly a part of the workscape of America. A
higher cost of living, increased mobility, and the need to use natural skills
are only some of the reasons. In spite of attempts to make the workplace
"gender neutral," however, women still face certain disadvantages—and
advantages—in the work force.

When a working woman undergoes a job crisis, she faces many of
the same problems that a man does. Like the man, she suffers loss of self-
esteem, becomes angry and frustrated, and may grow bitter because of
her situation. Like her male counterpart, she wants to be happy in what

she is doing. She needs to know how to find a better or different job. Also like the man, she may suffer burnout or get fired or laid off.

Increasingly, many of the job opportunities open to men are available to women as well. This is one reason in most chapters I discuss working men and women together.

Women, however, are not identical to men. Nor are their job opportunities always the same. Accordingly, this chapter addresses specific ways a job crisis can affect women. My comments are generalizations; they will not apply to every woman or every employment situation. However, they are based on interviews with a number of women, and therefore represent most situations.

REASONS WOMEN WORK

A common truism is that a man's identity is tied up with his career. Like many truisms, this one isn't universally true, but it is true of most men. Among the most common ice-breaking questions that men ask each other are "Where do you work?" and "What do you do for a living?" Men eventually ask such questions as "Are you married?" and "Do you think three-piece suits are ever going to become fashionable again?" But they rarely begin with those. Men work not only to make money but to gain a sense of personal worth, to build up a sense of identity, to *accomplish* something with their lives.

Although some women are as career-oriented as their male counterparts, most are not. (This includes many "career women.") Why, then, do they work?

After earning a teaching degree, Vivian Braun taught elementary school for two years in a small Nebraska community. But then her career direction began a series of changes. During her next eight years she worked at a Lake Tahoe resort and then as a sign painter's assistant in Hawaii, finally buying the business. Soon Vivian longed to return to her roots. She sold her business and came home to Lincoln. For two years she worked in a hotel restaurant. When the hotel cut back on its staff, Vivian lost her job. After being unemployed for nearly a year, she finally found a job as a travel coordinator for an auctioneering firm.

Now in her forties, Vivian explains why she didn't stick with teaching and use her college degree. "I really never looked on teaching as a career. It was just something to do, just a way of making money to survive. As a matter of fact, until I returned to Lincoln, I never gave much thought to having a career. And even then, it wasn't until after I got laid off from my restaurant job that I even thought of doing something permanent. In a sense, what I have now is a career. But I'm certainly not committed to doing it the rest of my life."

Ruth Wisniewski, an English graduate from Temple University and the mother of three children, is a part-time freelance writer. Ten years elapsed between graduation and marriage. An additional three years passed before the birth of her first child. During this period of thirteen years, she held jobs as a recreation director, a substitute teacher, a VISTA worker, a temporary office worker for Manpower, an assembly line worker, a secretary at a Christian school, a mother's helper, and a clerical staff member at a hospital. She lived in almost every section of the country —the East, the South, the West Coast, and finally the Midwest. Her sojourn even included an eighteen-month stay in the Middle East.

"I never had a sense of commitment to finding a good-paying job," says Ruth. "I certainly never thought in terms of a career. In the back of my mind, I always figured that some day I'd get married and have a family. Basically, I worked to survive until that day came. I kept a job until I tired of it. Then I moved on to something else. I'd probably still be changing jobs every six months to a year if I hadn't gotten married and had children. I'd probably have found much more of my sense of identity in serving people through volunteer work than in any job."

Gwen Vanderbeek, a bright, articulate woman in her early fifties, is single and probably will remain that way. "I've long since given up hope that my knight in shining armor will come along," she says.

Gwen has worked in the loss department of a major insurance company for more than thirty years. She is presently a supervisor of one of the areas within the loss department and is responsible for twelve people.

I know my opportunities for advancement are limited here, but that doesn't worry me. There are things more important than career advancement or making money."

"I suppose you could consider me a career woman," says Gwen, "but I don't look at myself this way. I have a job that keeps me financially comfortable. And it keeps me in contact with other people during the day. But it's also something I don't have to worry about on evenings or weekends. I'm pretty active in the church and in a couple of community organizations. I really think my identity is taken up much more with these things than with my job. Also, I have family in the area—my mother, a brother and sister, and their children. I stay pretty busy with them as well.

Vivian, Ruth, and Gwen typify the attitudes many women have toward work. For a woman, work is a means to an end. Many single women see a job as a temporary measure, something to do for survival until they get married and start a family. In contrast, single mothers may regard their work situation as more permanent. Still, their primary motivation is making sure that their children have a roof over their heads and food to eat.

For other women, work may be a social outlet. Work is where their friends are. They might even forego the chance at a better job or a promotion for the sake of remaining with the network of friends they have built up over the years.

Still other women see work as a means to service. Deb Hoak worked at one organization for two years before joining the marketing department of a Christian publishing house. She has worked there for thirteen years.

"I know my opportunities for advancement are limited here," she says, "but that doesn't worry me. I've had the opportunity of applying for jobs in other organizations, but I see what I'm doing as a form of ministry. All things considered, I'm really quite satisfied right where I am. There are things more important than career advancement or making money."

Granted, these are generalizations. Some women are as career-oriented as their male counterparts. But, on the whole, women work for different reasons than men do. This has its effect on the opportunities that are open to them.

DISADVANTAGES IN APPLYING FOR CERTAIN JOBS

Women are at a disadvantage when applying for certain jobs. Whether one calls it prejudice, stereotyping, or merely a pattern of hiring, women face limitations when applying for certain positions.

"When I was laid off from my restaurant job, I decided to see if I could find a career-type job," says Vivian Braun. "I went to employer after employer, begging for something—anything—in which I'd be able to advance. *Nothing* materialized. Employers don't want to take a chance on training a woman. They're afraid she's not going to stay long enough for it to be worthwhile."

Ruth Wisniewski adds, "If you're a woman looking for a job, a prospective employer is going to think that you'll be getting married a few years down the road. If you are married, they'll figure you will soon take time off to rear a family. It's hard to persuade them otherwise. Even with affirmative action, employers have a prejudice against women in careers."

Marge Salas is a single mom with a teen-age daughter to support. Despite her college education, she has mostly worked at low-paying jobs. She is presently a purchasing agent for a nonprofit organization. This is the best job she's ever had.

"Before I became a purchasing agent, I worked as a retail sales clerk. Prior to that, I was a substitute teacher. And before teaching I did various odd jobs, none of which lasted more than a few months. I've never really tried to get a more professional job. Not only didn't I think employers would find me qualified, but in most of the places I worked, I noticed that women rarely if ever advanced beyond a certain level. I pretty much gave up hope of moving up the ladder where I worked.

"Moreover, most of the time I had a growing daughter who demanded my attention. I simply couldn't satisfy the demands of a high-powered job. Nor could I take the time to go back to school for further training."

Maybe [there] is a bit of prejudice a prospective employer has against you as a woman. But it's the reality of the situation and something you have to live with."

A woman facing an employment crisis will find the going much tougher if her goal is to find a more professional job or locate a job with the opportunity for advancement. Like it or not, the prospective employer's presumption is that she is not going to last. Therefore, he is much less willing to invest time and energy in training her for a career-track job. This realization may itself be an employment crisis for some women.

There are, however, important exceptions to this rule. Not all employers are men. Some businesses and corporations are run by women. Others have women in powerful positions in the corporate structure. In these organizations, women have as good a chance of advancing as men —perhaps even better.

Moreover, in certain professions, a formally trained woman stands an excellent chance of rising to the top. Among these are law, accounting, college teaching, and medicine. Most colleges and universities take affirmative action very seriously. About the only levels not amply staffed with women are the highest administrative positions. Even at this level, things are changing. More than ever, women are filling positions as college deans, vice-presidents, and even presidents.

Law firms are also eager for bright female lawyers. While traditionally a male field, the legal profession presently has many practicing female lawyers. Although most senior partners are still men, this is bound to change as more women pay their dues as junior partners.

"If I have one bit of advice for a woman who wants a professional career," says Vivian, "it's to get training. Without it, you're going to go nowhere. *You* have to prove to an employer that you're serious about your career. Otherwise, you won't even be regarded as a prospect. Maybe that *is* a bit of prejudice a prospective employer has against you as a woman. But it's the reality of the situation and something you have to live with."

LOW-LEVEL JOBS

Women are more readily employed than men. This may sound almost contradictory to what you have just read. It isn't. There are more low-level jobs, and women are often placed there first.

"I've had tons of jobs in my life, and I've never had any trouble finding work," Ruth Wisniewski says. "I just didn't set my sights too high. Think of it. The number of high-level jobs is really small compared to the low-level jobs. Clerical jobs, retail sales jobs, secretarial jobs. There's millions of these out there. And if you've ever looked around, you'll see that most of them are filled by women.

"These jobs take minimal training. An employer is more than willing to hire someone who might work for only a couple years. He doesn't have to spend those first two years training the person. That same employer would go bankrupt if he had to pay the sort of salary a male head of household is going to require. He'll gladly pay a lower salary in exchange for a short-term commitment.

"Moreover, he knows that a man, especially if he's career-oriented, isn't going to be satisfied with one of these jobs for very long. Most of these positions are dead-end. The employer almost assumes that only a woman will want to work in a job like this, and so he hires accordingly."

"There's another factor," adds Molly McCourt, a retired personnel director. "Men in the work force want authority and recognition. I've seen this time and again. They get frustrated in jobs that don't offer these things. Moreover, men tend to be single-minded and achievement-oriented. They need a job that allows them to see a single task through to completion.

"Women tend to have a different set of strengths and needs. They don't need recognition nearly as much as they need the feeling that they've *served* someone through their job. And they're not single-task oriented. They are much more adept at juggling a variety of tasks all at once, putting aside one if another needs attention, not getting frustrated if a particular task doesn't get done according to their predetermined schedule, and so forth.

"Now what I've just described for you is a secretary or perhaps a project or travel coordinator. People who fill such jobs need juggling skills. At the same time they can't be concerned about a lot of recognition," McCourt explains. "When I was a personnel director, I hired women for these positions not because I thought that women were, for example, better typists or had a more pleasing phone manner. I hired women as secretaries, say, because I knew they had the particular strengths a secretary needed. I also knew that the typical man wouldn't be content very long as a secretary, not because he'd feel demeaned in the position, but because the constant juggling of various tasks would drive him crazy.

"From my experience as a personnel director I'd say that the number of positions that require the sort of skills women possess far outnumber the positions that require male-oriented skills. They may not be the glamor positions. They certainly aren't the ones that get a lot of recognition. Nor do most of them pay all that well. But there are a lot of them out there."

The bad news for women who are going through a job crisis is that there is still prejudice against women in certain careers and in many top management positions. The good news is that it's much easier for a woman to get a new job. This is especially good news for a woman who has lost her job. The chances are that if she's willing to take what's available, she will have a job much more quickly than her male counterpart.

STARTING CERTAIN HOME-BASED BUSINESSES

Women have a definite advantage in setting up certain home-based businesses. This is another piece of good news for women going through an employment crisis. If you are willing to start a home-based business, you may have a greater chance of success than men. This is especially true when running a professional service out of the house. Women who have a marketable skill and desire to stay at home can take heart in this.

When Barb Leeman had her second child, she gave serious thought to quitting her job as an accountant and staying at home. However, her husband persuaded her to go back to work, arguing that they needed her full-time income to make ends meet. Six months later, he walked out on her, suddenly and without warning.

As Barb began to pick up the pieces of her life, she decided she wanted to stay home with the children if at all possible. As part of the divorce settlement, her former husband, who was now living with another woman, was required to pay child support. The monthly payments, however, were not enough to permit Barb to simply quit her job. She needed another source of income. After mulling it over for some time, Barb decided to set up an accounting service in her home.

"The people at the firm told me it wouldn't work," says Barb. "They said there's a prejudice against a home-based professional—sort of like he or she is not *good* enough to work for a firm. But I really wanted to be with my kids, so I went ahead anyhow.

"I built up a decent clientele almost right away, and the number of clients keeps growing. There are those who seem to be a bit uncomfortable coming to my home for business. But most of them accept the arrangement. I really haven't noticed the prejudice my former colleagues warned me about. Ultimately, what counts is that I do a good job. Anyone who uses me once knows this."

"I don't know whether I'd get away with this if I were a man," says Stephanie Clark, who runs a consulting firm from her house. "I really think women have an advantage in starting a home-based business. Traditionally, the man has been expected to go out to work. The woman at home is more accepted. Clients overlook the apparent lack of professionalism. You're a woman. You have a reason for being at home. Therefore, you can be good, professional, and reliable, and still be working out of your house. Of course, it's really just a prejudice, but it's there nonetheless."

REENTERING THE WORK FORCE

Most men do not face the problem of reentering the work force after an absence of many years. Women often do. It's not unusual for a woman to marry shortly after completing her schooling, take off twenty or more years to rear a family, and then decide to return to work. The decision is sometimes forced upon her.

Sandy Robinson was forty-eight when her husband asked for a divorce. They had been married for twenty-eight years. During that time, Sandy had never worked outside the home. With their youngest of three children already in college, Sandy knew that she wasn't being left with a family to support. Still, she needed to find a job to provide for her own welfare. But what could she do? She had two years of college credits and no work history, other than a few part-time jobs that she held before she got married.

"When Rick left, I desperately needed a job," she says, "but my work history was practically nonexistent. I envisioned my résumé with my name, address, and telephone number at the top and one word underneath: "Housewife." Hardly the sort of résumé that would make an employer sit up and take notice.

"But then I got to thinking. In the previous twenty-eight years, I had done a lot—a whole lot. I had cooked and baked. I had kept my home immaculate. I had managed to keep three kids on schedule, making sure they got to school, Little League practice, music lessons, dance classes, and so forth on time. I had counseled them on just about every conceivable issue. I had kept a checkbook balanced.

"And that was just the start. I had served in various capacities with several volunteer organizations. I had been publicity chairman for a couple of them. I had served as treasurer on at least three separate occasions. I had been chairman of fund drives. I had even helped to write and edit a newsletter.

"The more I thought of it, the more I realized that I had a really impressive résumé, if I just emphasized the right things. Rather than mention my employment history—there wasn't anything to talk about—I decided to emphasize my skills. That's just what I did. So I wrote my résumé, listing all the things I could do and had done. Only later, during a job interview, did I find out this sort of résumé had a name—the functional résumé.

W omen who have been out of the work force for a long time have skills. . . . The important thing is identifying those skills.

"Personally, I wasn't concerned with what it was called. I started sending it out to various companies that had job openings. Believe it or not, I got three interviews. The third company that interviewed me hired me to be part of their promotional staff. I guess they figured that if I could promote myself so well, I could promote them too."

Women who have been out of the work force for a long time have skills. In fact, they may have developed a wider variety of skills than some of their career-oriented sisters. The important thing is identifying those skills.

If you are in the position of wanting or needing to go out to work after many years away from the work force, do what Sandy Robinson did. Ask yourself: "What have I done at home all these years? What skills have I gained? Of what organizations have I been a member? What offices have I held? What skills did I acquire while serving in these capacities? What are some other skills I've gained over the years?" As you answer these questions, you'll be surprised at how talented and marketable you are. Whatever you come up with, put in your résumé. You'll find that you're quite employable after all.[4]

You will also need references. You won't have employers to recommend you. But don't worry. Over the years, you have worked with many people. If you've taught Sunday school, your pastor or Christian education director will be able to vouch for your diligence and reliability. If you've been active in the local chapter of the PTA, its president can testify about your performance on various committees. Other members of service organizations in which you've been active can write a recommendation based on your work on fund-raising drives, publicity campaigns, newsletters, and the like. True, these aren't references from employers. However, if your prospective boss is not going to pass you over because you haven't been in the work force, he's not going to eliminate you because of these references either.

The woman returning to the work force after a long absence faces many obstacles. But she also has many opportunities. As more and more women return to work after taking time off to rear their families, those opportunities will continue to expand. They are there for you to take. You need only to know where and how to look for them.

PART **3**

COPING WHILE SHUFFLING

8

Living Without a Paycheck

Our Volkswagen Rabbit hummed steadily as we drove down Cornhusker Highway toward the Lincoln city limits. We were arriving just as an early-spring thundershower was about to hit. Elizabeth and I had been married just over one month, and I was eager for her to see my home town. I also wanted her to see the house I had bought six years earlier, the house in which we would now live as a happily married couple. I was happy. The rain that started pouring as we turned onto 84th Street could hardly dampen my enthusiasm for the moment.

After dining at Red Lobster, we drove to our house. It was small but cozy. And, although our belongings were still packed, we settled in for the evening. That's when it hit me. I was unemployed. So was Elizabeth. Neither of us had a regular paycheck coming in. For that matter, neither of us could be assured of earning so much as a dime. Suddenly I felt a pang of anxiety. What had I done? I had dropped out of seminary, gotten married, and convinced Elizabeth to come out to Lincoln on the promise that I'd make lots of money selling cleaning products. Now, here we were. No job. No income. Nothing. Just an uncertain, scary future.

Elizabeth and I lived without a paycheck for nearly six months. Yet, we managed. Eight years later, when I left the ministry, we managed again. This second time Elizabeth had a paycheck, but it wasn't enough for a family of four to feel comfortable. We managed on both occasions, however, because we followed several basic principles of surviving when the paycheck is cut off.

The four survival techniques I will suggest in this chapter are not just for the unemployed. You can use them if you are scaling down from two incomes to one. You can even use them if you simply want to live more economically, even if you are not anticipating an income reduction.

However, if you are unemployed (or about to be), these techniques are especially relevant. Unemployment is frightening. I don't want to minimize that. But it seldom creates a truly desperate financial situation. Even after your unemployment compensation runs out, you can and will survive. (I have been unemployed twice for long periods of time. I have never received a penny of unemployment compensation. However, God has allowed me to survive quite well.)

Here, then, are the techniques.

STAY OUT OF DEBT

If you're already in debt, the request to stay out of debt may sound like closing the barn door after the horses have fled. Perhaps. But you still need to follow this advice. You need to keep from getting further into debt. And if at all possible, you must reduce your outstanding debts. This may mean selling certain items you're presently buying "on time." You must be ruthless about this. *The less debt you have at this time in your life, the better*.

If you're not presently in debt, avoid accruing debt. This is not the time to purchase a car, a video cassette recorder, a new television set, or anything else if you can't afford to pay cash for it.

Personally, I would give this advice to anyone at any time, even those with stable jobs. Deficit financing creates a day of reckoning down the road. You cannot predict the future with any certainty. You don't know when a financial reversal will put you in a position where you won't have money to pay your creditors.

One reason Elizabeth and I have been able to survive our periods of unemployment is because neither of us have ever had a penny of debt. In fact, for the first nine and a half years we were married, we didn't even own a credit card. We do now, but we have it for a specific purpose and we use it judiciously. (Momentarily I will discuss the advantage of owning a credit card—*if* you're able to use it wisely.)

Debt's burden can be devastating. Consider Frank and Joe, both age thirty. Frank earns $2,500 per month while Joe makes $2,000. They each have a wife who doesn't work outside the house and two children. Frank has always bought things on time and presently makes payments of $500 a month on various items. He also owes $700 per month on his mortgage —or $1,200 altogether. Moreover, Frank keeps the balance on his credit card near his credit limit of $4,000. Frank's take-home pay (after taxes and payroll deductions) is $2,000. After paying $1,200 to his creditors, he has $800 left for all other expenses, including the minimum he must pay on his credit card. Needless to say, he doesn't save much. In fact, Frank doesn't even have a savings account.

Joe, on the other hand, has never bought anything on time. Because he saved enough for a down payment and bought a modestly-priced house, his mortgage payments are just $550 per month. Joe owns a credit card, but uses it sparingly. He always pays the total credit balance each month. Joe's take-home pay is $1,600. After paying on his mortgage, he has $1,050 left. For years, Joe has been able to put $400 a month into savings.

When Frank and Joe both lose their jobs, who suffers more? Though Frank earns $500 a month more than Joe does, he must find $1,200 *before* he even thinks of putting bread on his family's table. If Frank falls behind, he risks having his car and other items repossessed as well as losing his house. He will also get a bad credit rating. In a word, Frank is in a bind.

Joe, on the other hand, must find $550 each month for his mortgage, plus whatever is necessary to provide for his family's basic needs. Interest from his savings will take care of some of those needs. He can come up with the remainder by withdrawing from the principal. Times won't be easy for Joe, but he'll be years ahead of Frank. Do you see why debt is so bad?

You may already be in debt. If you have a job, start in earnest to pay off the debts. Don't acquire any new debts. If possible, start saving on a regular basis. Do this today—not next year, not next month, but *today. Get out of debt at all costs.*

As I've already noted, if you've lost your job, do whatever possible to get rid of your outstanding debts. Sell what you are buying on time and

Four Strategies for Financial Survival

The following strategies, described in detail in this chapter, will help you to survive any financial difficulty, including loss of a second source of income and loss of unemployment payments. They require your active involvement, of course, but they are realistic action steps you can take now.

1. *Stay out of debt.* If you are not in debt, do not add to your expenses by borrowing. If you are in debt, get out of debt at all costs. You may sell unnecessary extras—a second car or television set. (See Strategy #2 below for other selling strategies.) You certainly should sell any consumer goods you are buying on time to cancel those loans.

Credit cards should be used only when cash funds are available to repay the charge *in full* each month. Do not borrow to purchase items for which you cannot pay.

2. *Sell what you can.* Be creative in selling items of value that are not essential. This may include specialized collections, old but little read books, knickknacks, and unnecessary furniture and appliances in good condition. To decide what items go on the selling block, ask yourself, "Do I really need this item?" If you answer no, let it go.

The best selling places are local dealers for your collections and classified ads for appliances, vehicles, and large pieces of furniture. A front yard or garage sale is a good approach for selling less valuable but interesting household items and books.

3. *Save whenever possible.* Snacks, minivacations, and a new cassette may seem to be good ways to reduce stress during these tough times, but they don't reduce your budget. Scrutinize your spending habits and cut out the extras. To reduce the food bill, be a coupon clipper and eat most meals at home. Go to maybe one nice restaurant a month instead of three fast food stands a week.

Be sure to look for sales to buy the essentials at the best possible price. However, postpone clothing purchases as much as possible. When clothing is necessary, consider thrift stores and garage sales for used clothing, and end-of-the-season

Four Strategies (cont.)

clearance sales at department stores for new clothes. (You may pay one-half the original price at clearance sales.)

4. *Do odd jobs.* Part-time jobs offer variety and tap into your present and buried skills. You set your hours (between your job search and interviews) and probably will find a variety of locales. Odd jobs can include baby-sitting, house-sitting, painting houses, doing repair work, delivering papers or telephone books, and typing. Though such jobs may be sporadic and will pay only modestly, they will bring in money when you need it and may be enough to get you over the hump.

pay off the loan. Sell that extra car, television set or whatever else you're buying on time. You may take a small loss today, but you'll be far ahead in the long run.

What about credit cards? There are some practical advantages in owning one. First, if you travel long distances, you don't need to take along enormous sums of cash or travelers' checks. Moreover, if your car breaks down and needs major repairs, you're not stranded. Second, you build up a credit rating, which is important if you plan to buy a house someday; a credit rating is essential for obtaining a home mortgage.

Despite these advantages, we still would have said no to a credit card if we hadn't been sure that we could handle one responsibly. And I wouldn't advise anyone else to get one unless he or she can do the same.

To use a credit card responsibly, you must resolve to do two things. First, you must resolve to buy with your credit card only what you can pay for with cash. If you don't have the money today, don't use your credit card. Second, you must resolve to pay the entire credit balance by its due date. (In fact, the best thing is to keep your money in an interest-bearing account until right before the due date and then send in your payment. In this way, the interest you gain between time of purchase and payment will more than offset your annual credit card fee.) If you can't abide by these two resolutions, cut up your credit cards—or don't get any to begin with.

SELL WHAT YOU CAN

Elizabeth and I could not have kept our budget during the first six months we were married if we had had to depend on my savings alone.

We also generated sorely needed cash by selling various things. Here's a list of the major items: (1) old baseball cards; (2) silver coins given to me by my aunt years earlier; (3) a gold bracelet Elizabeth had bought in Saudi Arabia; (4) a class ring; (5) a machine to measure friction; and (6) numerous old but nearly unused books, including the complete writings of the church Fathers.

These items brought in approximately $2,000 altogether. We have never regretted selling any of these, except the baseball cards. The ones we sold increased in value at least tenfold. On the other hand, the price of both gold and silver has gone down drastically in the past decade. As for the writings of the church Fathers, well, I opened a volume once the whole time I had them. I can't say I've missed them. And anyone who buys a friction-measuring machine in the first place has to be a little bit crazy.

We didn't succeed with everything we tried to sell. Elizabeth had some Venetian glass (valued at approximately $1,000). No one seemed the least bit interested in this particular item. Otherwise, our sales were successful

If you're living without a paycheck (or are scaling down to a single income), you need to consider this second strategy. Whether you make $500 or $5,000 this way, the money will come in handy. The approach is simple: go through your possessions, evaluate their worth, and as appropriate sell them through one of several ways.

Any article in good condition—collections, antiques, extra vehicles, furniture, and appliances, for instance—is saleable. Ask yourself, "Do I really need this item?" If your answer is no, put it on a list marked "Items for Sale." Then review your list, asking three questions about each item: "Will it decrease in value or stay the same over time? Can I sell it for more than fifty dollars? Is there likely to be a buyer?" Put items that elicit three yes answers at the top of your list. They are the ones you want to sell first. Items that are likely to increase in value over time (such as old baseball cards) you should sell as a last resort. You can use a garage sale for items you can't get much for or are difficult to sell.

Where can you sell these items? You have several alternatives, including through a dealer, classified ads, and a garage or yard sale. A dealer is probably the best alternative for selling coin or stamp collections or antiques. You won't receive top dollar, but you will get rid of them quickly.

You can place an ad in the classifieds or tack up a notice on a public-service bulletin board. This is probably your best choice for selling appliances, vehicles, and large pieces of furniture. It also may be a good way of selling a sports card collection, particularly if you want to sell it bit by bit.

You can have a garage sale. Because most people who attend garage sales expect to spend only a few dollars, this is probably not the place to sell your more valuable items. However, you should sell fairly quickly those items worth less than fifty dollars. You can also put out your hard-to-sell items, on the off chance that someone will be interested.

Finally, you can use word-of-mouth advertising. Let your friends at church or in the neighborhood know that you have certain items for sale. They may be interested.

SAVE WHEREVER POSSIBLE

Let's look in again on Frank and Joe. Frank spends ten dollars a week on lottery tickets. Fran, his wife, averages five dollars per week. Each day Frank buys at least two cans of pop from the canteen, a series of vending machines at work, and usually buys a candy bar or two as well. Often he stops by a McDonald's or Taco Bell for lunch. Fran doesn't like to cook, so Frank takes the family to Bonanza or a pizzeria a couple times a week. Fran doesn't have time to clip coupons or look for sales. When she shops, she usually gets whatever the family has run out of. If she's in a hurry, she'll shop at the nearby convenience store.

Joe doesn't play the lottery. He enjoys an occasional pop, but he buys it on sale at the store and keeps it in his refrigerator. Before he lost his job, he used to bring a sack lunch. Now he eats at home. Dinner out is a special treat. The family goes to a restaurant once every couple months. Jill, his wife, is a fanatical "coupon clipper" and comparison shopper. She knows the lowest price she can expect to pay on almost every item the family needs. She waits until a store puts an item on sale. Then she stocks up.

The month before Frank and Joe lost their jobs, Frank's family spent $500 more on "the necessities" than did Joe's. That $500 differential is going to make a big difference now that they're both unemployed.

Frank and Joe represent the two extremes. However, if you want to survive without a paycheck, you will have to live a lot more as Joe does than as Frank. Moreover, you won't learn new habits overnight. Thus the time to start is now, even if you're not unemployed. You don't know what the future will bring.

The following ways to save money are not exhaustive. Your own creativity can add many others. These seven suggestions, however, will save you a considerable sum each month. If you want to survive without a pay-check, you'll *have* to implement most of them.

First, *avoid those canteen snacking areas.* Many people drop two to three dollars in change into them each day without realizing it. If you do this just five days a week, over the course of the month you'll spend an additional $45 to $65. Small change adds up. If you must have candy and pop, buy it in quantity when it's on sale at a store. There's no sense help-ing to pay for someone else's machine.

Second, *if you play the lottery, stop.* I don't say this because of any moral issues. (I think the lottery is morally wrong, but that's secondary.) The lottery is expensive and unnecessary, especially for the person with-out a paycheck. Ten dollars a week adds up to $40 a month ($50 on those extra long months). You don't need to waste your money in this way. This comment applies to other vices—such as smoking—as well.

Third, *eat at home as much as possible.* Lunch at a typical fast-food restaurant will cost an individual about three dollars. A family of four may be able to get by on ten or fifteen dollars. Many restaurants are considera-bly more expensive. Even at some "family restaurants" the bill can run as high as forty dollars.

Suppose you eat your own lunch at a fast-food restaurant three days a week and take your family out for lunch each Saturday. And suppose you treat your family once a week at a Bonanza-style steak house. You'll spend at least $160 a month. If you ate all these meals at home, you wouldn't spend more than $40 (probably less). You'd save over $120. If you enjoy taking your family to dinner, do it once a month at a really nice restaurant, resolving to spend no more than $50. You'll still be $70 ahead.

Fourth, *clip coupons.* You may have to buy the Sunday paper to do this. The investment is well worth it, however, if you clip the coupons *and* use them.

Using them is crucial. Clipping coupons is a worthless exercise if they stay in the drawer when you go to the store. And they're no good if they have expired. Every week before I shop I go through my stack of coupons. If I have an item on my list for which I have a coupon, I take it. I also look for coupons that are about to expire. If I don't have a coupon for that item with a later expiration date, and I know I'll use the item eventual-ly, I'll add it to my list.

Using coupons *wisely* is equally important. Don't buy something you don't need just because you have a coupon. You're wasting your money if you do this.

It's impossible to say just how much you'll save by clipping coupons. My personal experience is that we save somewhere between $35-$45 per month.

Ham and Turkey

An easy yet novel way to save money and thus stretch your budget is to buy extra meats at the holidays. For instance, hams are usually on sale around the holidays. Slice some for your first meal and for sandwiches. Use some for scalloped potatoes and ham. Keep some to flavor homemade pea soup. Freeze some for later use.

Turkey is another bargain. I regularly purchase several turkeys right before Thanksgiving. They are extremely reasonable then. Sometimes stores will actually give them away with a purchase of, say, $75 in groceries. We keep several in the freezer. From time to time throughout the year we prepare one.

From one bird we get five or six regular turkey meals, two meals of soup made with the carcass and neck, and four or five meals of creamed turkey.

Ham and turkey, often thought of as a Thanksgiving, Christmas, or Easter treat, can last much longer than the holidays if you buy several on sale and store them in the deep freeze. They will taste just as good when you prepare them weeks, even months, later.

Fifth, *shop for bargains.* This doesn't mean always shopping at the discount food store. It does mean faithfully checking the ads of various supermarkets. It means studying these over a period of time, determining what items regularly go on sale and what items don't. It means coming to have a good idea of what is the rock-bottom price on any given item.

We visit regularly two supermarkets that double the value of coupons. If I have a coupon for a particular item, I'll almost always use it at one of these two stores. The price I pay is generally less than what I'd have to pay at the discount market. However, I shop at our local discount market for items that never go on sale and for which I never have a coupon.

How much more would I spend on food if I didn't shop for bargains? I can't give an exact figure. My educated guess, however, is that the difference is almost $100 per month.

Sixth, *put off purchases of clothing* as much as possible. If you have growing children, you will have to buy some clothes, but you don't have to pay top dollar. Visit garage sales and thrift stores. If you do shop at department stores, wait until the end of the season when clothing goes on sale. Often you will pay half or less of the original price.

Seventh, *plan your trips.* Do several errands on one trip. If you don't do this, you may wind up taking a couple extra trips each day. This uses up gas, and gas costs money.

For instance, I'll generally make two shopping trips each week. I make sure that I'm getting everything we need so that I won't have to make an extra trip. Moreover, I shop on the way home from dropping Annie off at school. I do this because I can stop by the grocery store without having to go significantly out of my way. I stop at the post office on my way to UPS. If I need photocopies, I wait until I need to go downtown and stop where photocopies cost only three cents per copy. By using the car judiciously, I save a tank of gas per month.

Some of the savings I have suggested are small. Some are fairly significant. Combined, they add up to a savings of several hundred dollars per month. When you're living without a paycheck, that's a lot of money.

WORK PART-TIME JOBS

Although neither Elizabeth nor I drew a paycheck the first six months we were married, we weren't exactly idle. We tried to start a business selling cleaning products. That failed miserably. But we did generate income in other ways. We cleaned apartments at five dollars per hour apiece. When we both worked eight hours a day, we made eighty dollars. It was dirty work and was far from steady, but at least it generated some income.

I took in typing. Here too the work was very sporadic. But it was more pleasant than cleaning apartments, and it yielded a few hundred dollars each month.

One of our more unusual jobs was "mystery shopping." Many business establishments will pay people to be mystery shoppers. All the mystery shopper has to do is patronize the establishment and then fill out a form evaluating the service he or she received. Elizabeth became a mystery shopper at a fast-food Mexican restaurant chain and at our local bank. Some months she made as much as $75. That may not sound like a whole lot, but when you're unemployed, every little bit helps.

Incidentally, most establishments have trouble getting and keeping mystery shoppers. So ask around. Many fast-food restaurants, banks, and retail shops (including department stores) need mystery shoppers. Sometimes they will advertise this need right on their premises or in a classified ad in the newspaper. If you don't find advertisements for mystery shoppers, phone the personnel departments of places you think might need them. (That's how Elizabeth got her "job" with the bank.) Or ask your friends. Some of them may be mystery shoppers. Almost anyone qualifies as a mystery shopper. All these establishments ask is that you patronize them enough to make it worth their while.

If you become a mystery shopper for several establishments, you can easily make over $100 a month this way. (Also, you'll be able to eat at a fast-food restaurant without feeling guilty for spending your money. Order a small soda and hamburger. You'll spend a little over a dollar, and you'll get paid five dollars for your efforts.)

Part-time jobs abound. You can mow lawns, deliver papers, distribute flyers, paint houses, do repair work, baby sit, or house sit. If you can't find enough work this way, you can use temporary employment services, such as Manpower. You're almost certain to find intermittent work through them. These jobs won't bring in the income of a full-time job. But at least you'll be bringing in money at a time when you desperately need it. What you make in this way may be just enough to get you over the hump. Moreover, you may learn a secondary skill that will prove helpful in landing a full-time job down the road.

Living without a paycheck is never easy. As I said at the outset, it's scary. But the situation isn't desperate—not if you follow the above strategies. Follow each one faithfully, and you should be able to weather your period of unemployment. And, really, that's all you need to do until you find another job. You won't get rich. But neither will you go broke.

9
What About the Children?

"When I found out Wehrmeyer's was going to lay people off," says Jeff Swanson, "I was really upset. I wondered whether I would get another job, whether Sue could find something while I was out of work, whether we'd get all our bills paid. You name it. The things unemployed people worried about—I worried about them all. But one thing I never gave much thought to was how being unemployed would affect our children—Becky, Ben, and Allison."

"Becky and Ben were already in school," adds Sue, "and I had Allison enrolled three days a week in a preschool program. I assumed that because they were out of the house so much of the time, the change wouldn't affect them all that much. Jeff had always been good with the kids. I figured he knew how to get lunches ready and entertain them in the afternoon. So, even if he was at home and I was at work, I didn't think things would be all that different."

Sue found a job shortly after Jeff was laid off, so he began to watch the children. Though he did an adequate job, Jeff never told his children the reason he was at home, and they seemed confused by it, especially the two younger ones. "Maybe it was because they were younger, but they never really adjusted to relating to me as 'mommy.'"

"Children—especially young children—require a lot of patience." Jeff noted. "I'd get really frustrated when Ben or Allison would make a mess or wouldn't eat their breakfast as fast as they should. Sometimes I'd get really angry when I'd be interrupted while doing the housework. Maybe moms have these reactions as well. But I know that had it been Sue, she'd have had a much higher level of tolerance.

"Thankfully, I found another job after about four months—just before summer vacation started. I still remember what Ben said when he found out that Sue would be home. His very first comment was, 'Great! We're going to have the real mommy home again.' I suppose if I thought I had been a good 'mommy,' I'd have been hurt. But I'm sure he was right. I'm not as good a mommy as I am a daddy."

When a job crisis results in a role reversal, the children are affected. Daddy isn't Mommy. (For that matter, Mommy isn't Daddy.) A job crisis, however, can affect children in other ways as well. Unemployment can result in children sharing their parents' humiliation when they have to admit that "Daddy (or Mommy) is out of work." To them, their parents' loss of income can mean that suddenly they don't have all the things to which they've become accustomed. They may also be affected by the emotional tensions of a job crisis.

This is what Scott Manwarden found out. Scott never lost his job, but he *did* go through an employment crisis. The crisis began when he realized that he was stagnating in his career as a computer programmer. His family was affected in ways that he never could have imagined.

Reflecting on what happened, Scott says, "I was really consumed by my own problems. I hated my job. I wanted to try something new—brand new. And all I could think about was what I, Scott, was going to do. I had always been open to Mary and the children. I became closed. I had enjoyed playing ball in the evening with the boys. I loved going out to the lake on weekends, fishing and swimming with the children. Then I started withdrawing into myself. All I could think of was my frustrations with my job. I just didn't have the time or energy for my family."

After several months, Scott's wife finally confronted him. They had planned to attend a weekend family retreat with the church. But on noon Friday, Jeff called Mary from work and told her he wanted to stay home that weekend. "I felt exhausted from my job and from all the struggling I had been doing.

"When I got home that evening, Mary was ready for me." Jeff says. "She started recounting all the times in the past few months we had canceled out of something at the last minute. She had quite a list. Then she went on to say that I was becoming a total stranger to the kids, that I never did anything with them anymore, and that I was cheating them out of having a father. She climaxed her tirade by letting me know in no uncertain terms that if we didn't start doing things as a family, she would do things with the kids and would leave me to be miserable by myself.

I set aside one evening per week and at least a half day every weekend to do something special with my family."

"I realized right then and there that something needed to be done. But what? I really didn't feel I had the energy to do anything with the kids, or with Mary for that matter. At the same time, I had always prided myself on being a good husband and father and wanted to remain one. I knew that I had to do two things. I had to resolve my job crisis. And I had to be far less consumed by it in the meantime.

"We went to the retreat that weekend. I can't say I enjoyed myself immensely, but I tried very, very hard to be attentive to my family. From then on, I made it a policy to think about my work problems as little as possible except when I was on the job. I also set aside one evening per week and at least a half day every weekend to do something special with my family. Thankfully, a few months later I was able to make a career switch. I was re-energized by my new job, and this spilled over to my family as well. Once again, I felt I could give them the attention they deserved."

Wayne Levin exudes confidence. You would never guess that he has gone through a job crisis. But he has. In fact, he has been unemployed for over three years. Or, as he would say, he hasn't had a "traditional job" during that time. The way he dealt with his crisis shows how the negative aspects of a job crisis (such as economic hardship and loss of self-esteem) can be turned into something positive.

Wayne was a college history teacher who was denied tenure. He knew the job market in the humanities was bad. Moreover, he had really grown fond of the town where he and his family had lived for seven years. Therefore, he made the decision to try to find work locally rather than looking for an academic position in another part of the country. Wayne's search was futile.

"Time and again I was told that I was overqualified," says Wayne. "I could never quite understand this. All I wanted was something to put bread on the table. But eventually I began to believe what everyone was saying. I decided I was never going to get a job working for someone else. My only alternative was to do something on my own."

With an artistic bent and an enjoyment in photography, Wayne tried to make it as a freelance graphic artist and photographer. He also considered himself "a pretty decent writer," so he began to submit pieces on local color and popular history for various magazines. He knew, though, that he would not have steady work right away. "The first two years we really struggled. Even with ViAnn's job as a bookkeeper, we could barely make ends meet.

"Our children suffered at first," Wayne notes. "We really had to scale back financially. This meant that they had to wear garage sale specials, hand-me-downs, and Salvation Army retreads. We stopped taking them to McDonald's and Pizza Hut. We couldn't even afford to go to Mr. Donut's on Saturday morning. And we had to cut out piano and trumpet lessons. Our two oldest, Peter and Jed, were most aware of the change, and they squawked the loudest.

We also had to deal with what the kids told their friends I did for a living. I didn't want them to feel ashamed that I was unemployed.

"But the whole time we tried to be up-front with our children and emphasize the positive. They knew that our newfound poverty was only temporary. And we tried to involve them every step of the way in what we were doing. I was even able to train Peter, who was already in his early teens, to help with the developing of my photographs. This way, he felt like he was part of our family enterprise.

"We also had to deal with what the kids told their friends I did for a living. I didn't want them to feel ashamed that I was unemployed. We were up-front with them, and we wanted them to be up-front among their friends. At the same time, the word *unemployed* has a stigma attached to it in our society. We solved this dilemma by using the phrase 'traditional job.' Our children's friends learned that I didn't have a traditional job, but that I was still extremely busy doing what I was doing—managing the household and doing my photography, my graphic artwork, and my writing. I don't know whether their friends understood, but it gave our children a sense of pride in their household and their father.

"I think that as a result of the way we handled it, we have a really enthusiastic family today. My business is their business. They want to see us succeed as a family every bit as much as I do. And we have a unity that's seldom found in families nowadays."

A job crisis *is* a family affair. From listening to what Jeff, Scott, and Wayne have said, we can see that children are affected in various ways.

THE ECONOMIC IMPACT

If a dad loses his job or a mom loses hers, the family suffers economically. Unless it has saved up a considerable sum of money or has other major sources of income, the family will have to cut back on its spending. It will have to put on hold the purchase of major household items, clothing, and various "extras." Children may find that they have to wear cheaper, out-of-fashion clothes. They may be forced to wear hand-me-downs from their older siblings. In extreme circumstances, they may even have to make do with mended shirts and pants and shoes with holes in them.

A job crisis is a family affair. ... Prepare your children for the change in their lifestyle.

Whereas at one time, Mom and Dad could take them out to eat, they now find themselves eating all their meals at home. The extra treats are missing. Cheaper cuts of meat replace the more expensive ones. Peanut butter and jelly become a staple at lunchtime. Birthdays and Christmases, which at one time were celebrated with much festivity and many presents, now seem bare. Each child receives one or two presents, if even that. Many of their expectations, fueled by the surfeit of previous years, are dashed.

Younger children may not notice these changes, but older ones will. If a job crisis is going to mean a loss of your income, it's important for you to prepare your children for this change in their lifestyle. They should be given some idea of what to expect. You should tell them that certain things will be cut out, and, as much as possible, tell them what those things will be. Make sure that your children know that these are not being taken away as a form of punishment. At the same time, they should be reassured that, as soon as possible, those things will again become a part of family life.

You should also do all you can to not let it appear as though *everything* is being taken away. If you've been accustomed to going out to McDonald's with your children, make sure you still do so. You don't have to go out as often or order as much, but don't cut this out from your children's lives completely. If possible, don't totally eliminate that new item of clothing or that surprise present. You may not be able to get the more expensive item any longer. You may even have to scour garage sales or the local thrift store, but you should still do what you can to make your children feel like they are getting something new and that you care.

The more you can make the economic impact upon your children less obvious the better. They'll have enough to worry about without having to be concerned about their food and clothing.

THE EMOTIONAL IMPACT

A job crisis is often a time of anger and frustration. Husbands and wives are likely to be much more on edge and may explode at each other and at their children with little if any provocation. I have seen this happen time and again in our own family. When I was going through my own job crisis, I tended to react with hostility to any slight, real or imagined. If Elizabeth expressed anything about me that I could possibly interpret in a negative way, I did so. An innocent remark could easily lead to a blow-up. Our children were often bewildered and frightened.

Anger isn't the only problem. Scott Manwarden withdrew from his family. This is another common reaction during a job crisis. Mandy Haynes, a single mom with a fourteen-year-old daughter, can testify to this.

"When Lollard's department store closed its doors, I lost my job as a sales clerk. For several months I was without full-time work. I found that communication with [my daughter] Erin pretty much broke down. Until then, we had always been open to each other. But I was so consumed with my own problems—looking for work, wondering how we'd make ends meet, feeling sorry for myself—that I didn't have time for hers. And as a teenager, she was right at the age where she *especially* needed someone to talk to. Only when she made a feeble attempt at suicide by swallowing some pills did I realize that I was no longer being the mom she had always turned to for so many years."

Many children are too young to understand that "Daddy (or Mommy) needs to be alone." All they know is that the love and affection they used to receive are missing. Teenagers, such as Erin Haynes, may find their mom or dad distant at the very time they most need them to be close. Granted, Dad or Mom may love their children every bit as much as they always have, but they're not expressing it. To children, this makes all the difference in the world.

We may think we have good reason for our indifference to those around us. But our children don't understand. They may think they have done something wrong.

Like Scott Manwarden and Mandy Haynes, I showed this cool response to my children while unemployed. When I was alone with our children the entire day, I didn't mind taking care of them, but at day's end I needed to be alone. Elizabeth would return from work and say, "Let's go to a movie tonight, just the two of us," or "Let's all go to Valentino's for dinner."

Immediately I'd resist. I'd say something like, "Not tonight. I'm just too exhausted," or, "I'd just as soon stay home. It's always too crowded on Friday nights." Whatever the occasion, I had an excuse.

Invariably, I'd had enough social interaction—and particularly interaction with the kids—for the day. In retrospect, I can see that I must have seemed distant and uncaring to Annie and John.

We may think we have good reason for our anger or our indifference to those around us. But our children don't understand. They witness that anger. They feel that lack of love. And they may think that they have done something wrong. They haven't. But we must make sure they *know* they haven't. We can do this only if we're especially sensitive to them during our job crisis.

THE SHIFT IN PARENTAL ROLES

Young children may not be aware of a change in the family's economic condition. They are, however, very much aware of the role reversal that often accompanies a job crisis.

Jeff Swanson found out that he wasn't "Mommy." I know this as well. I'm a fairly competent "homemaker." I know how to do the laundry. I can cook. I'm a pretty good baker. I can dust, vacuum, scrub floors, and clean the bathroom, though I don't particularly enjoy these jobs. I can't sew or hang curtains, but I know plenty of women who can't do these things either. If this were all that was involved in being a "mommy" to the kids, I'd be a pretty good one.

But it's not. Men rarely have the ability or desire to provide the tender nurture that children receive from their mother. This may not be a very popular thing to say in this day of the blurring of sexual roles. But it's true. Daddy may give his attention to the kids, but it's not Mommy's attention.

I f you convey a sense of shame, embarrassment, or guilt, your children will feel the same way.

A role reversal, whether temporary or permanent, will have an effect on the children. Dad and Mom must both be aware of this. Dad must be more sensitive than he's ever been. He simply *must* be available to the children, even if he feels like totally immersing himself in his tasks. He must listen to them, take time to read to them, play games with them, and give them a spontaneous hug now and then. Even if she's tired, Mom must continue to be "Mommy" when she's home. If anything, she should be even more mothering than she usually is. Only in this way will the children receive the tender nurturing they sorely need.

THE CHILD'S ESTEEM

When a person loses his job, he may lose his sense of dignity as well. That person's spouse and children may also be affected. A wife may feel humiliation when she makes the admission, "My husband is unemployed." And even children, particularly when they are old enough to understand the expectations of society, may be ashamed to admit that their father or mother is out of work.

If you're going through a job crisis, you need to be sensitive to the fact that your children may share your sense of shame. It's been said that one of the first thing men say to each other when they meet is, "Where do you work?" Kids don't ask quite the same question, but they *do* say, "My daddy's an accountant," "My mommy is a sales clerk," or "My daddy drives a truck." What does a kid say whose daddy or mommy is unemployed—"My daddy (or mommy) doesn't do anything"?

Or what if your daughter's school teacher gives the class the assignment of describing what their parents do for a living? How is your daughter going to feel when she has to begin, "My daddy is unemployed" or "My mommy is out of work"?

Be sensitive to the fact that your children may be placed in a position where they suffer the same embarrassment and shame you feel. You need to discuss your situation with your children. If you convey a sense of shame, embarrassment, or guilt, your children will feel the same way.

On the other hand, if you realize that your situation is not one for which you should feel embarrassment or shame, your children will pick up on this. You can explain to them, for instance, that millions of others are in your position, that men and women have times when they must go through an employment adjustment. You can even do what Wayne Levin did; you can tell them that you are not working in a traditional job. However you explain it to your children, they should not see your situation as one about which they should be ashamed.

Remember, kids, particularly those in junior high and high school, have enough trouble with their self-image without having to feel guilty about their parents' employment situation. That's why it's crucial to explain what you're going through in as positive a way as possible.

THE POSITIVE EFFECTS

A job crisis can rip families apart. It can also draw them closer together. Honesty before your children and asking them to help in little ways can foster true family unity. This is particularly true of families that take an employment crisis as an opportunity to start a home business. Typically, everyone in the family can be involved in this enterprise in some way or other. It becomes an adventure in which all participate. As Wayne Levin found out, this creates unity in the family.

Suppose you don't want to start a home business. Suppose you just want to get a job as fast as you can. Or suppose all you want to do is find a job you can love. You can still make this a positive experience for your children.

This is what Dawn Rogers did. Dawn was a high-school graduate with three children. After being widowed at age thirty-two, she took a job in a food-processing plant. She also enrolled at a local community college, where she took evening courses in commercial art.

"I really despised working at the food-processing plant," says Dawn, "and that hatred grew with every passing week and month. For whatever reason, I didn't get a job as a graphic artist as quickly as I thought I would. I was frustrated. But I received continual encouragement from my children. And I involved them in my job search. Meg, my oldest, typed all my job applications. Jim, who was a freshman in high school at the time, kept all my applications neatly in a file. Even Peter, my ten-year-old, got involved. He made a chart, with my help, on which he kept track of all my applications, how many were still 'live,' whether I had gotten an interview, which ones were no longer viable, and so forth. I really feel we drew closer together as a family through this.

"And, of course, we prayed. Just about every night we prayed that the Lord would give me the *right* job—the one He wanted, not necessarily the one I would have chosen. Finally, when I got a job as a commercial artist, it was almost as though we had *all* been hired. That's how unifying an experience it was."

I was actually overwhelmed by the response of my family. ... The positive attitude they had ... carried me through."

Dave Borth was also able to turn his job crisis into a positive family experience.

"Before I lost my job, we never did much together as a family. However, when I got laid off, I knew we'd have to do a lot of belt tightening. The night after I found out, when I had finally recovered from the shock, I gathered the whole family around the kitchen table. I told them that we were all in this together and that we needed cooperation from each one of them in economizing and in finding little ways here and there to make money.

"Almost immediately, Alan said that we should each keep a record of how much we were able to save each day. He volunteered to actually keep a daily log for the family. It figures. He's always been conscious of money.

"Chad volunteered to get a paper route. Pris said that she'd bake cookies and sell them at school. Anna, my wife, had some money-making schemes as well.

"I was actually overwhelmed by the response of my family. At first, I wondered if their enthusiasm would last. After all, it seemed rather incongruous. Here I was, out of a job, and everyone was having a great time. But, you know, the positive attitude they had at the beginning carried through. In fact, it carried *me* through. There were times I would have broken down because of frustration and discouragement. But to see my whole family pitching in really helped."

As the cases of Dawn Rogers and Dave Borth illustrate, a job crisis can be a positive experience for the family, including the children. But, again, it boils down to attitude. If your attitude is positive, if you seek to involve your family in a positive way, your job crisis will build family unity. Otherwise, it won't.

And, of course, there is prayer. The old saying "The family that prays together stays together" is especially true during an employment crisis. If you pray through your job crisis with your family, your family will be built up in its love for one another and for God. You can count on this.

10
How Do You Cook Meat Loaf?

*M*onday morning. Bill Fredrick hears the alarm's buzz on the far side of the bed. His wife, Sally, fumbles briefly before she hits the switch. *Why'd she set her alarm?* Bill wonders, still half asleep. Then he remembers. *Sally starts work today.*

Three weeks earlier, Bill had lost his job as an assistant manager at Kressler's department store. When Kressler's closed because of declining sales, Bill had been let go. He started applying for jobs, so far without success.

So Bill and Sally reached a decision. Sally had worked as an accountant before their first child came along. She would look for a job and work until something developed for Bill. Bill would stay home and manage the household, which included Danny, a second grader, Linda, who was in preschool, and Charlie, a busy two-year-old. There was also Bridgette, their Irish Setter, and an assortment of goldfish.

Bill's body cried to stay in bed that Monday morning. He had gotten used to getting up much later. But Sally's first day at her new job would be Bill's first day as a household manager, and he wanted to get off to a good start.

As Sally showered, Bill prepared breakfast. In a few minutes the coffee was brewing, the boxes of cereal were on the table, the orange juice was poured, toast was in the toaster, and his and Sally's places were set. Bill's debut was humming along smoothly.

At seven o'clock sharp, Sally left for work. Now Bill had exactly one hour and fifteen minutes to serve the children's breakfast, make Danny's lunch, and get everyone dressed and piled into the car. Bill figured he could give himself at least fifteen minutes to read the morning paper.

That proved to be a mistake. He hadn't counted on spending extra time making oatmeal for Linda ("I have oatmeal *every* day") and trying to find where Sally put the carrot scraper ("Mom always puts carrot sticks in my lunchbox," Danny insisted. "Where's my carrots?"). Changing Charlie's soiled bedding took time also, and Bill did not realize how long dressing Linda and Charlie would take, especially bundling them in their coats, hats, and mittens.

Finally, at 8:25, he drove the three children to school. Bill had anticipated a ten-minute drive, but stops for school buses and heavy traffic almost doubled the time. At 8:45 their car pulled up in front of Danny's school, and his seven-year-old made a mad dash to his classroom.

Because Linda's preschool didn't start till 9:15, Bill had planned to stop at Super Saver, which was right on the way, to do the grocery shopping. That is what Sally always did. There was just one problem. In his haste, Bill had left the shopping list on the kitchen counter. However, since he had the time, he decided to stop anyway and get the items he could remember.

Sally had always done most of the shopping, so Bill was unfamiliar with where items were located in Super Saver. Between trying to remember just what he was supposed to get and hunting the unfamiliar aisles, Bill lost track of time. When he got to the check-out counter and finally glanced at his watch, he recoiled in horror. It was already 9:20! Linda would be late for sure.

When Bill returned home with little Charlie, he checked the shopping list to see what items he'd forgotten. All things considered, he hadn't done too badly. However, getting ground beef for that evening's dinner had totally slipped his mind. He would have to stop again when he picked Linda up from preschool.

Bill was midway through putting groceries away when he remembered that he had to do the laundry. Sally had told him there were at least three loads. With Charlie's soiled sheets, that could easily be four. Bill figured he'd better get right onto this next task.

With the first load in the washer, Bill decided to take care of the dusting. This took a bit longer than he had expected. Moreover, he had to stop several times to attend to Charlie's needs and to transfer wash to the dryer and reload the washer. It was nearly noon and time to pick up Linda when Bill remembered that he hadn't finished putting the food away. Rushing into the kitchen, Bill discovered that the ice cream was already beginning to leak through the bottom of the paper sack, the frozen orange juice was completed defrosted, and the gallon of milk was at room temperature. Hurriedly, he put food into the refrigerator and cleaned up the mess left by the melted ice cream.

Just as he was about ready to take the load of permanent press clothes out of the dryer he discovered that Charlie had a badly soiled diaper. The diaper changed, Bill hustled Charlie into the car. He knew he was already late for Linda, so he decided to get the clothes out of the dryer when they returned. Once again, he forgot his shopping list. Super Saver would have to wait until he picked Danny up at three o'clock.

Back home, Bill got Charlie and Linda settled at the kitchen table for lunch. He then headed to the laundry room where he discovered that the term "permanent press" is a bit of a misnomer. All his shirts and Linda's blouses were badly wrinkled from staying in the dryer far too long.

Afternoon went more smoothly. Bill finished the laundry and folded it, picked up Danny on time, got the rest of the food at Super Saver, and got home in plenty of time to start dinner. Sally would be home at five o'clock. Bill figured that if he started dinner at 4:30 he could have the food on the table by 5:30.

At 4:30 sharp, Bill stopped playing Candy Land with Linda and headed toward the kitchen. Sally had told him to make meat loaf with the ground beef. *Meat loaf*, Bill mused. *How do you cook meat loaf? Well, this shouldn't be too difficult. I'll just look in a cookbook.*

Bill soon had a recipe in front of him and was happily preparing the ingredients when his eyes lit on the words "cooking time: 1 hr. 15 minutes in oven preheated to 350°." *That sure is longer than I expected,* Bill thought, glancing at his watch. It was already 4:45.

Just then, Charlie awoke from his nap, howling. Bill rushed into Charlie's bedroom. Charlie pulled himself onto Bill's lap and clung to him. Ten minutes later, Charlie had gotten over whatever had frightened him and Bill put him down. Hurrying into the kitchen, Bill turned on the oven and finished preparing the meat loaf. Just as he was putting it in the oven, Sally's car drove up. Supper would be at least forty-five minutes late.

With Sally home, Bill recounted his first day as household manager—both the triumphs and the defeats. His lack of planning had made Danny late to school and Linda late to preschool. Moreover, Sally's blouses and his shirts were all in need of pressing. But he had made three meals, done the laundry, and dusted the house. He was utterly exhausted, but he had survived. Above all, he had learned some important lessons in *time management.*

Bill's experience is typical of someone thrust into an unfamiliar environment. Some tasks will go smoothly. Others won't. Some jobs will take far longer than expected. Others will be a snap. Whether you're a dad at home for the first time or a wife or mom who's worked outside the house until now, there's an art—and challenge—to being an effective household manager.

Many unemployed parents will save money on child care and housekeeping by doing it themselves. This chapter should make the task a little easier. Though not a how-to manual of home economics, this chapter provides several helpful hints. If you follow them, the transition to your new environment will be much smoother.

Three elements are essential to becoming a good household manager: time management, task management, and people management.

TIME MANAGEMENT

The summer after I graduated from high school, I held my first "real" job. I worked in the loss department of an insurance company in downtown Chicago. The first few days I was there my boss gave me a very limited number of tasks to perform. They took me all day. In a week or so, these tasks took no more than a couple hours.

The same pattern was repeated when I went into teaching and again years later when I entered the ministry. At first, the most basic tasks (for instance, preparing lectures, sermons, or Bible studies) consumed most of my time. Within a few months I had gained sufficient skills to spend much of my time attending to other duties.

When a person begins a new job, he or she will be relatively inefficient at the tasks that must be performed. As time goes on and he becomes more adept, he can do these tasks more quickly. Moreover, he will learn that certain tasks can be "streamlined." That is, he learns that he can take shortcuts or even eliminate certain steps without negatively affecting the outcome.

How To Manage Your Time at Home

Time management at home need not be complex. Three simple steps for organizing your limited time for a variety of tasks are schedule, combine, and eliminate.

First, *schedule your tasks.* Stick to a schedule whenever possible, and you will accomplish much in little time. Begin with a written schedule, allowing extra time initially.

Second, *combine your tasks.* Typically you can do two or three related tasks at once. These related tasks will be apparent as you see similar activities occurring throughout the day that could be coupled together. For instance, you can handle several errands with the car during one trip.

Third, *eliminate the extraneous.* Don't allow other tasks to interrupt what you are doing; do the secondary tasks later. Rid yourself of distractions, and you will accomplish much more.

Managing a household is no different from any other job. As you become more accustomed to what you are doing, you will find that you can perform your tasks more efficiently and streamline your work. However, the secret of being fully efficient is time management.

Time management is a science in and of itself. Seminars and books have been devoted to it. Time-management consultants are hired by companies to increase the efficiency of the work force. Efficiency in the home is equally important, for that is your workplace during this time. Here are just a few essentials for managing your time in the home more wisely.

Schedule Tasks

First, you must learn to *schedule tasks.* One of the greatest detriments to using time efficiently is not having a schedule. People who wake up in the morning without having any idea what to do waste a great deal of time figuring out what tasks to tackle that day. And, if you go through your day without a clear idea of what you will be doing next, you'll find that you fritter away precious moments and even hours simply deciding what to do.

Granted, you must be flexible. That is particularly true if you have small children around during the day. Still, you need to stick to a schedule as much as possible.

Here's one example of how scheduling can help you do much in a short period of time. Every morning before I wake up the children, I make the lunch that Annie will take to school. While I'm at it, I also make the sandwich I'll give John at lunchtime. Because I have the carving board out, I prepare the salad for dinner. On Tuesdays and Thursdays I have a load of laundry in the washer while I'm doing all this. On Mondays I take out the trash so we don't miss trash pick-up.

By now it's time for me to awaken the children. It takes me approximately three minutes to prepare their breakfast. While they're eating, I either fold laundry or draw up a shopping list. Next, it's time to drive Annie to school. However, because I have my shopping list, I can shop on the way home. In a period of a little over two hours, I've accomplished quite a bit.

If you desire to work efficiently at home and not be overwhelmed by your tasks, you must schedule them. You may want to start with a written schedule. If this is your very first time as a household manager, you may not know what all your tasks will be. But you will know some. Unless you're rich enough to hire a maid (in which case, you're probably not reading this book), you'll have to dust, vacuum, do laundry, shop, cook, and take out trash. If you have children, you will have to take care of their needs and make sure they get to school. If you own or rent a home, you'll have to find time to mow your lawn, rake leaves, and tend your garden.

You may have little idea how long these activities will take, so leave plenty of time, particularly at the start. It's better to have a little time left over at the end of the day than not enough time. The important thing at the start is *having* a schedule. So go through the list of things you know you'll have to do and start filling in your schedule. For instance, schedule laundry for Monday and Thursday mornings. Use Wednesday or Friday morning for shopping. Clean the house on Tuesday. And so forth. (Make sure you leave time for cooking every day.)

You also should leave extra time when an obligation requires that you do something at a specific time. The unexpected is bound to turn up. (I don't know how many times I've been interrupted by an important phone call fifteen minutes before I *have* to be somewhere. Having a time cushion makes me far less nervous.) Above all, don't try to cram too many tasks, however small, into the time just before you have an unbreakable obligation.

Combine Tasks

A second and related aspect of time management is the coupling of tasks. When Annie started going to school, I prepared her lunch in the morning and made John's at noon. I made the salad right before dinner. However, all three of these tasks require my being in the kitchen and they all use the carving board. It makes more sense to couple them. By doing them at the same time, I save a considerable amount of time overall.

When I first managed our household, I went shopping whenever I felt like taking a break from being in the house. But then Annie started school. Almost immediately, I started shopping on the way home from dropping her off. Coupling these activities allowed me to save both time and gas.

To a certain extent, you won't know what tasks can be combined until you actually start managing your household. However, you should always be on the lookout to see what sort of tasks require you to be in the same area of the house (or town) and use the same or similar equipment. For instance, you may have several errands to run outside the house, such as getting a child to school or a Little League game, stopping for groceries, picking up stamps or mailing packages, and buying a birthday present. Combine your errands and do them with one trip. You'll save considerable time this way.

Eliminate the Extraneous

Third, successful time management also requires the elimination of the extraneous. Put another way, you need a single-minded devotion to the task at hand. You will accomplish your tasks much more efficiently if you don't let yourself get distracted by other matters. Sometimes you will be interrupted by events beyond your control. (Small children are especially good at doing this.) You can't help these interruptions. But you can eliminate self-created interruptions.

If you're in the middle of scrubbing the kitchen floor, don't start dusting. If you're drawing up a shopping list, don't write out a check for the electric bill. If you've started a batch of cookies, don't decide to tighten a loose doorknob. Work on the task at hand and bring it to completion.

Above all, don't let yourself be interrupted by distractions such as soap operas, magazines, crossword puzzles, and the like. If you think you must take a break to watch television, read, or call a friend on the phone, wait until you've completed the task at hand. That task will take much longer if you have to come back to it and start again. If you find you *can't* work long periods of time without a break, schedule your breaks into your daily routine. For instance, set aside a half hour in the afternoon for your favorite daytime television program. (But keep it to that one program!) Or, spend an hour reading a book or a magazine in the morning. But don't let such things disrupt your household tasks.

TASK MANAGEMENT

Closely related to time management is task management. (As a matter of fact, they are overlapping concepts. Time management is nothing more than doing your tasks in a way that makes efficient use of your time. And task management is managing your tasks in a way that allows you to save time doing them.) Task management involves planning tasks, organizing tasks, the orderly execution of tasks, and streamlining tasks.

You must first plan your tasks. If you have made a schedule (either on paper or in your head), you have already begun to plan. However, you must also plan the detail. For example, if you decide to bake, you must decide what to bake (perhaps a pie, a cake, cookies), how long it will take (some items require a lot more time than others), what recipe to follow, and so forth. If you are going to do laundry, you have to plan how much laundry you want to do, what sort of laundry (coloreds, whites, permanent press, etc.), and whether you want to fold and put away the clean laundry or save this for a later time.

Next you must organize your tasks. If you decide to do the laundry, you must gather and sort the clothes, find the laundry detergent, the fabric softener, and perhaps the bleach, and decide what settings on the washer and dryer are appropriate for your loads. If you want to cook a meal, you need to know what utensils you are going to use, have them on hand, and figure out how long various parts of the meal are going to take so that they are all completed at approximately the same time.

You must then execute your tasks in an orderly fashion. For instance, if you're cleaning your house, you should do it room by room. If you're weeding your garden, you should go row by row.

Finally, you must start streamlining your tasks. At first, you won't know how to eliminate the extra steps that make your tasks cumbersome. But as time goes on you will learn how to combine steps and cut certain corners without the quality of your work suffering.

Let's now take these ideas and show how they can be applied to certain household tasks. We'll consider three areas—cooking and baking, laundering, and cleaning. But be forewarned. This is not intended as a complete household manual. You can find these in a bookstore or the library if you're interested. I will simply offer a few suggestions that can start you on your way to becoming a good household manager.

Cooking and Baking

Cooking and baking are not mysterious art forms. They are really straightforward tasks that anyone can master with a little work.

First and foremost, you need a cookbook. Whether you are making something as simple as meat loaf or as complicated as a spinach souffle or a red velvet cake, you will have to follow a recipe.

You may already have one or two cookbooks, perhaps as a wedding gift. If so, use them. If not, buy a fairly comprehensive cookbook, such as *The Joy of Cooking*, by Romauer and Becker (Bobbs-Merrill). If you want to economize, I'd suggest you get a copy of *The More With Less Cookbook*, by Doris Longacre (Herald). This cookbook contains many recipes that use leftovers and is an excellent source for meatless main dishes. It's one of the most-used cookbooks in our house.

If you decide to get into baking you will want one or more cookbooks devoted primarily to breads, cookies, cakes, coffee cakes, pies, and the like. For some tips in using the cookbook as a starting point to wholesome cooking, see "Cookbook Creativity" on the next page.

Baking is also surprisingly easy. Just remember to follow the recipe and measure accurately. I'd suggest starting with cookies. Bar cookies (such as brownies and chocolate chip bars) seldom take more than fifteen minutes to whip up. Spread the dough in a greased pan and place in the oven and you are well on your way to a tasty treat.

Cooking and baking are a good example of how important it is to organize your tasks if you're going to manage them efficiently. You need to know what utensils and ingredients you need, where you keep them, and how long it will take to bake or cook the dish you're making. Bill Fredrick had problems with something as simple as carrot sticks because he didn't know where the scraper was. And nothing can be more discouraging than starting a chocolate cake only to find that the tin of cocoa is completely empty. So, before you start, pull out your utensils and ingredients and organize. It will save you time and may even prevent a minor disaster.

Laundering

Laundering provides a good example of the importance of planning your tasks. You need to know how to divide the laundry into different types of loads, what setting is appropriate for each sort of fabric, and how long a typical washing and drying cycle takes. Bill Fredrick was doing well with the laundry his first day as household manager until he ran out of time and couldn't get the permanent press fabrics out of the dryer promptly.

If you haven't done so already, familiarize yourself with the washer and dryer you will be using. Most washers will allow you to wash in hot, warm, or cold water. Many washers give you the option of washing in hot or warm water while rinsing in cold. With today's powerful detergents, you shouldn't ever have to use hot water to wash your clothes. Warm or cold water works just fine. I always use cold water for the rinse cycle.

Cookbook Creativity

Some think that cooking by the book ruins creativity. But cookbooks are simply guides to assure that you know the basics in every category. You certainly can improvise after you learn the basics. In addition, every cookbook has its own special recipes that put refreshing twists on old stand-by meals. When you buy a cookbook, you will have all the basics for baking, broiling, and frying.

Here are three guidelines to remember for creativity:

1. You should follow the directions the first time around. The instructions are generally easy to follow. Many cookbooks have glossaries to explain terms to the novice. Once you know the basic idea for a meat or side dish, you can free lance, giving the dish a personal touch.
2. A local butcher can tell you the best way to prepare a particular meat. Many cuts of meat are simple to prepare. All you need to know for many roasts is how long to cook them and at what temperature.
3. A simple meat can be dressed up by the toppings you use. For instance, chicken can be flavored with barbeque sauce, a marinade, several seasonings, such as sage, marjoram, thyme, and seasoning salt, and even with fruit (pineapple is an unusual but winning topping). Serving chicken a different way each time gives variety and makes it seem that you are offering a new meat at the evening meal.

Many dryers have settings marked for different types of fabrics (e.g., "sturdy/cotton," "permanent press," "knits/delicates"). This is helpful, and more useful than "high," "medium," and "low," the settings for some dryers. In general, the higher the temperature, the shorter the drying time. However, the higher the temperature, the harsher treatment your clothes receive. You should always dry your permanent press and delicate fabrics on a low setting. If you're not sure of what setting to use, it's best to err on the side of caution.

Now to the clothes themselves. You're probably familiar with the old bromide about separating the whites and the coloreds. It's still good policy. While many fabrics today don't run, some do. And the only way you can know for sure is to take a chance—or wash each colored fabric by hand in hot water the first time you wash it. (If no dye is released into the water, the garment can be washed safely with white clothes.) Even a seemingly innocuous item sometimes offers a surprise. Recently, we washed John's green Ninja Turtles pajamas for the first time. I'm now sporting my first pair of pastel green undershorts. (I don't take responsibility for this one. Elizabeth did the load.)

Even more crucial is the type of fabric you do in a given load. Generally, I wash towels and washcloths together. If these don't make a full load, I throw in sweat shirts, T-shirts, and my running shorts. These things are best washed in warm water and aren't hurt by high drying temperatures.

Cleaning

I hate to clean. I hated cleaning when I was single. I hated it when I was cleaning apartments. I hate it now that I'm a household manager. Because I hate cleaning so much, I try to do it as quickly and efficiently as possible. Quickly and efficiently means often. If you clean before things get too dirty, you will find that cleaning goes more quickly. You'll also find that you'll detest it less.

You should *dust* at least once a week. Dusting requires a clean, slightly moistened cloth. Commercial dusting sprays (such as Endust) are available. A spray bottle filled with water works just as well. Start with the same room and the same piece of furniture every time you dust. Make sure you get into the corners of bookshelves and into any crevices in the furniture. Remove and dust under books, knickknacks, and pictures. Dust window sills regularly.

You should *vacuum* at least once a week as well. Vacuuming also requires planning and orderly execution. I find that the best way to vacuum is to do the whole house at one time. First, go through the house and pick up toys, papers, and anything else that's loose and on the floor. Next, do an entire room nonstop. If possible, do a couple rooms at a time. Repeat the procedure for the next area of the house. After you vacuum your house a few times, you'll get into a routine that works best for you. If you have a routine, you'll save time, and you won't mind vacuuming nearly as much.

Bathrooms should be cleaned at least once a week. The toilet and sink should probably be cleaned more often. For quick touch-ups, use a disinfectant cleaning wipe. For more thorough cleaning, use cleanser and a rag to clean the wash basin and the outside of the toilet bowl. Use a disinfectant to clean the inside. Apply a bathroom tile cleaner regularly, preferably every week. Tile floors also should be scrubbed regularly.

The *kitchen* sink and counter should be wiped each time they're used. At least once a day you should give them a thorough cleaning with a rag and warm, soapy water. This is one of the best ways to prevent the spread of disease through contaminated food. (Any time you prepare poultry, be especially careful to clean the counter. Chicken and salmonella are nearly synonymous.)

Remember, cleaning also includes picking up and straightening rooms. Often children can help with such chores, especially in their own bedrooms.

Keeping a house clean isn't easy. You may never grow to like it. But once you know how to do it and get into a routine, you won't hate it quite as much.

PEOPLE MANAGEMENT

Unless you live by yourself, you will be engaged in people management as well. You will have to take care of needs, coordinate schedules, and supervise tasks.

Your children have needs. So does your spouse. When your children are a bit older, taking care of their needs can sometimes wait. (This doesn't mean they're irrelevant. You must still attend to them.) When they're very young, their needs must often be met immediately. This can interrupt even the most well-coordinated schedule.

Many of the comments I've made about task management also apply to needs management as well, so here just a few additional ideas First, know what sort of needs must be met. If you have young children, you'll need to dress them, feed them, put them down for their naps, and change their diapers. You should allow time in your schedule for these things.

Remember, your children need your time. You should take time to play with them, talk to them, and do things with them (such as take them to the mall or the library). As household manager, it's your duty to make sure you don't neglect your children.

Similarly, take time for your spouse. Whether you're a busy mom trying to fit a hundred household chores into your daily schedule or a dad at home for the first time, don't neglect your spouse. He or she needs your companionship. He needs to use you as a sounding-board for his ideas. Therefore, set aside time just to be with your spouse.

People management is not just taking care of needs but coordinating *schedules* as well. If your children are extremely young, this may not be much of a factor. (To some extent, *you* determine when they will eat and nap.) But once they start going to school and become involved in activities (such as Little League or music lessons) your task as manager becomes much more complicated. You will have to plan meals and your other tasks around *their* schedules. You will have to know how long it takes to get from your house to the school or the ball diamond. You will have to know how to make last-minute changes when they don't tell you they have to be somewhere until fifteen minutes beforehand. You will have to become extremely flexible. And if they don't get where they're going on time, you will be responsible.

Finally, as household manager, you will have to learn how to *supervise* tasks. Your children need to learn how to help with the household chores. For the very young, this can be as simple as putting away their toys. But children also need to learn how to do dishes, keep their rooms tidy, make their beds, clean a house, and do the laundry. A good manager will delegate tasks. The older your children, the more tasks you can delegate to them. This teaches them the value of work and prepares them for adulthood. At the same time, it makes your task a little bit easier. Of course, you have to teach them to do things right. Remember, you are responsible for the way things are done.

Your spouse (even if he or she is working outside the home full time) needs to be involved in the household tasks as well. Most women, even if they are out working, will continue to help with the household tasks. According to one study, "A woman with a full-time job does 70 percent of household tasks, compared to 83 percent for her homemaker counterpart. Males do about 14 percent, regardless of job description."[5] Involving a working spouse in the household tasks is a crucial ingredient of making that spouse feel like an integral part of the home. This is especially important if the spouse is working outside the house for the first time.

Sharing tasks with your mate and children is an important ingredient in creating family unity. When all parties are involved in the work of the home, they will share in the sense of accomplishment that comes with having a well-managed household. In a time when so many families are falling apart, unity is a commodity to be cherished.

Managing a household is a difficult task. I should know. I've managed one for some time now. In the process I developed a true appreciation for the work that millions of "housewives" do every day, an appreciation I may not have gained otherwise. But a household is *manageable.* If you follow the suggestions I've made in this chapter, you'll be well on your way to managing yours.

11
ESPN, Soap Operas, and Other Time-Wasters

When Ben Novacek lost his job as a construction engineer, his wife went to work. He stayed home to care for their twin boys. This kept him busy for a while. But then the twins began kindergarten. Ben found he could do most household tasks in a couple hours. Because the twins were gone for four hours each morning, Ben usually finished the chores well before they came home. Sometimes he played ball with his boys for part of the afternoon. But by midafternoon they were tired. They came in and either watched television or took a nap. Ben had more free time than he knew what to do with.

Now and then, Ben tackled a home improvement project. He did some painting, and fixed up the family room a bit. However, the house was still relatively new and didn't need many repairs. As time went on,

Ben started watching television while he was alone in the morning. More often than not, he took a nap in the afternoon. He wasn't happy that he was wasting so much time, but he couldn't think of anything better to do.

Reading had never appealed to him. From time to time he thought of starting a home-based business. But all his ideas seemed like long shots, and so nothing ever really got off the ground.

A couple blocks down the street, Arnie Peterson was going through a similar struggle. Arnie was quite a bit older than Ben. He was in his late fifties and had lost his job when his company merged with a much larger firm. As a midlevel executive, Arnie had always had a good salary. His wife, Flo, had worked part time when their children were young. After they were grown, she worked full time for several years. Moreover, Arnie had made some wise investments. So money was no problem. Arnie decided that rather than look for another job at his age, he might as well retire.

After working long hours for thirty-five years, Arnie relished the thought of puttering around the house, taking extended vacations in their motor home, and spending time with his beloved Flo. For the first few months, this is what he did. He put in a patio, started a garden, and built a tool shed. He and Flo took a trip across the country to visit their children and some old friends they hadn't seen in years. When they weren't traveling, they'd spend a couple hours each day after breakfast lingering over a cup of coffee and chatting. Often they went out to lunch or dinner together.

But Arnie was still a relatively young man, and he needed a lot more to keep him occupied. He began to grow restless. He did some reading, but a couple hours a day was all he could take. He worked on crossword puzzles, but he soon became bored by these. For a long time he had thought of building a model railroad. So he went to a local hobby store, bought a few kits, some track, and a couple manuals. However, he lacked the patience for the detail work so crucial to model railroading. His kits, tracks, and manuals soon were collecting dust on the shelf. Arnie found himself at loose ends, not knowing what to do.

Meanwhile, Darla Bengtson, Arnie and Flo's married daughter, was facing a struggle of her own. Having moved from her native Wisconsin when she got married, she was now living with her husband, Brian, and their three young children in suburban Los Angeles. Darla had worked until their second child was born. That's when she decided to stay home with the kids. When their youngest was born thirteen months later, that seemed like a wise decision indeed.

But now, three years later, the oldest child was in school, and the other two were old enough not to need constant care. Brian and Darla didn't want to send them to preschool. Moreover, they were considering home-schooling their children a year or two down the road. Going back to work—even part time—was out of the question for Darla.

The children and the house, however, didn't begin to fill up Darla's time. Most of the younger women in the neighborhood and in the church where she and Brian were members worked during the day. Therefore, Darla didn't have many social contacts. The temptation to sit around and watch television or sun bathe by the pool in the back yard was great. And Darla succumbed.

Ben, Arnie, and Darla are typical of most people who spend much of their time at home. The unemployed or laid-off man or woman, the stay-at-home dad or mom, the newly retired executive all face a similar problem—what to do with their time. *Idleness* is one of the greatest problems confronting people who are not in the traditional work force. Though a stay-at-home parent may be caught up in a frantic schedule when he or she has little ones at home (as noted in the previous chapter), many who are home find they have too much time available.

If you've worked outside the house for several years, initially you will have plenty to keep you occupied. Things will need fixing. You'll catch up on your reading. You'll diligently send out job applications (if you're looking for work). Perhaps you'll visit friends or take a trip. You may spend time with your hobbies. If this is your first experience as a household manager, you'll be kept extremely busy while you get the hang of doing new tasks.

One day, however, you will wake up and have little to do. Because you will feel uncomfortable sitting around and doing nothing, you'll try to find ways to fill up your time. I know. I've been unemployed twice, and I've found plenty ways to waste my time.

Television is especially alluring. I've never cared for soap operas, and I'm more than happy to leave The Elephant Show and David the Gnome to my little boy. However, sports are another story.

The summer after we were married I practically wore out our television set watching sports on ESPN cable television. That was the year of the two-month long baseball strike. About the only sport worth watching was Canadian football. I've never followed the Canadian Football League, but that summer I watched just about every CFL game that ESPN broadcast. For one season I became an ardent Edmonton Eskimos fan and followed them to their victory in the Grey Cup that fall. The only reason I did this was because I had time on my hands and needed something to keep me occupied.

Even today, the temptation is there to waste time on sports. And I confess that when the Cubs' game is broadcast over WGN cable, I turn it on.

It's not just sports. Sometimes I'm tempted to sit in front of the TV set under the pretense of "wanting to be informed." During the Gulf War, I frequently kept the set on for hours at a time. And I've frittered away a morning now and then watching the House of Representatives over C-SPAN.

Television is just one form of temptation. I've known people who putter around their house, fixing one thing or another, painting a room, or dusting every day just to keep occupied. A person can take up a hobby simply to fill up the time. On occasion, I've opened and sorted baseball cards not because I've had to do so for my business but just because I wanted to have something to occupy my time.

Even reading can become a way of filling up the time. And I'm not just talking about reading "escape" literature. Reading informative books can be every bit a means of escape. I have always been an avid reader, not of escape literature but of theology and history books. Though such books may sound boring, you may be wondering, "What's wrong with reading theology and history?" There's nothing wrong with it. But when you're doing it simply to fill up the time, you're doing it for the wrong reason. During the times I've been unemployed, I've read many theology and history books. I haven't read all of them because I wanted to become better informed. Some of them were simply available and I had nothing else to do, so I read them.

Perhaps you're wondering, "If I don't have anything *better* to do, why shouldn't I waste my time in these ways?" The answer is simple: You do have better things to do. Therefore, when you find fulfilling ways to occupy your time, you will feel productive and avoid frustration. Here are several ways to utilize your extra time and not feel guilty about wasting time as you wait for a job or consider other options.

CONDUCT A THOROUGH JOB SEARCH

If you're actively looking for work, *making a thorough job search* is a worthwhile way to spend your time. As I indicated in chapter 4, looking for a job can be a full-time occupation in itself. However, that is a good way to spend your time only if you're really serious about finding another job.

Both times I've been unemployed, I have spent time looking through the classifieds and job listings in professional journals and have sent out numerous résumés. At times I was serious about looking for work. At other times I was simply filling up my time. If you're sending out résumés just to have something to do, you are better off watching television. If perchance you get called for an interview, your lack of real desire for the job will show through and you won't get hired. So use your time to conduct a job search only if you really want a job.

CONSIDER FURTHER EDUCATION

You might consider *going back to school*. Perhaps you have a desire to become an accountant, a lawyer, a baker, or an electrician. Now may be the time to pursue this interest. Again, do this only if you really want to be trained and if you intend to use your education. If you go back to school simply because you want to have something to do, you're still just filling up your time.

If you really do want to go back to school, you have several alternatives. You may consider enrolling in a college or graduate school program. To receive training in some areas, you'll have to do this. If you want to become a brain surgeon, you must go to medical school. A law degree requires a law school education. Before you enroll in programs of this nature, you need to count the cost—not just the financial cost, but the cost to your time and your family. If you live in a town that does not have the program you want, you will have to relocate. Even if a program is available at a local college or university, you must be willing to make a major time commitment for the next several years.

Community and junior colleges offer many worthwhile programs. You can enroll in courses in accounting, computer programming, business administration, electrical engineering, and a host of other specialties. Community colleges often cater to the adult population, so many of their courses are offered in the evening. This allows people with job and family responsibilities to enroll. Moreover, the tuition is usually quite reasonable. You can take a course in an area where you think you might have an interest without making a huge financial commitment. If you want to pursue matters, you can take more courses. If not, you haven't lost a great deal of time or money.

Correspondence courses are a third option. These allow you maximum flexibility. You can learn without ever having to leave home. However, be cautious. Make sure that you are dealing with a credible correspondence school. Unless you're taking the course entirely as a lark, be certain that you can receive college credit for your work. You never know when you'll need it. (Your local Better Business Bureau should have information on the various correspondence schools.)

PERFORM VOLUNTEER WORK

You might consider *volunteer work*. That is what Arnie Peterson finally did. Eighteen months after he retired, he started tutoring foreign students at a local high school. He had always enjoyed youngsters, so when he heard about this program through a friend, he figured it might be just what he needed to keep occupied. It was. He found the foreign students polite, eager to learn, and a real challenge to his communication skills. Several of them became his friends and even visited him and Flo after they graduated from high school.

Tutoring high school students is just one kind of volunteer work. Many programs would welcome volunteers to help the elderly, the disabled, and the hospitalized. Many charitable organizations need volunteer workers, as do political campaign staffs. The possibilities are almost endless.

In fact, the number of organizations that use volunteer workers is so vast that you may not know where to begin. I suggest that you narrow down the field before volunteering your services. What sort of work fascinates you? Are you most interested in working directly with people? Do you enjoy using the telephone? Are you more a "behind-the-scenes" person?

If you enjoy working with people, for what sort of people do you have a special burden? The elderly? The disabled? Disadvantaged youth? The sick? Are you especially interested in certain causes? Perhaps you have strong views on the environment. You may want to see more research done on a certain disease, such as multiple sclerosis. Maybe you have a special concern for the life of the unborn.

As you answer these questions, you will have a better idea what sort of volunteer work you want to do and for what group or cause. Contact the organizations that work with that group or for that cause. See if they use volunteers. If they do, volunteer your services.

Don't overlook your local church. Besides the obvious forms of service, such as teaching Sunday school, singing in the choir, or working with the youth group, there are many other things you can do. If you're a member of a small congregation and possess secretarial skills, your pastor might welcome your services as a part-time secretary. You might volunteer to do some needed repair work. Perhaps you can organize and run a church library. If you're at a loss for ideas, see your pastor and ask him what you can do. He will be able to offer many suggestions.

BEFRIEND SOMEONE IN NEED

You might consider *befriending a person in need.* That is what Darla Bengtson finally did. One day, when she was taking a walk with her preschool children, she noticed an older lady sitting in a wheelchair on her porch. Darla went up to chat with her. This lady had many health problems and was extremely depressed. Darla took a special interest in her. Whenever she needed medicine, Darla would get it for her. She often cooked meals or baked cakes or breads and brought them to her. If she needed to go somewhere, Darla would drive her. Darla got such enjoyment from doing this that she subsequently found two other older ladies in the area for whom she provided similar comfort and companionship.

You'll find needy people nearby no matter where you live. The elderly, the sick, the grieving, the single parent all stand in need of help and friendship. You may be the person to provide these things to a person or persons in need. All you must do to find them is keep your eyes open. You're sure to spot them.

BEGIN YOUR OWN BUSINESS

You might consider *beginning your own business.* Starting a business is never easy. It takes an idea, motivation, and patience. But if you have any inclination along this line, now is the time to begin (see chapter 13 for detailed information).

Ben Novacek had many ideas, but for a long time he lacked the necessary motivation. Shortly after he lost his job, however, he began baking whole-grain breads. He never thought of doing this other than for personal enjoyment. But one day a friend commented on their fine quality and mentioned that there was no place in town to get such a variety of whole-grain breads. Ben began to think about marketing his breads. His wife took several loaves to work where they sold immediately. Several coworkers asked for more.

With this initial success, Ben went to the local food co-op and a couple health food stores to see whether they would market his breads. The co-op and one of the health stores was willing. Word of Ben's breads spread, and he began getting more orders than he could fill from his own kitchen. Eventually, Ben rented a storefront, bought baking equipment, and opened his own bakery. While he still specialized in his whole-grain breads, he started baking other items as well. What started with a few loaves shared with a friend became a thriving business.

Before he had his own bakery, however, Ben had to start somewhere. You do too. Whether you decide to start your own business, go back to school, do volunteer work, befriend someone, or look for another job, you must resist the allure of idling away your time or filling it with unprofitable activity. It is very easy to fall into this trap and even convince yourself that you are using your time wisely.

Your time must be redeemed. And the way to redeem it is to start today. Turn off ESPN or your favorite soap opera. Don't play that extra game of solitaire. Put down that book you've been reading. (Put down this book, if necessary.) Look into a college program. Contact a volunteer agency. Find someone to befriend. Start planning seriously for your own business. Whatever you do, begin today. Tomorrow might be too late.

PART 4
TRANSCENDING THE SHUFFLE

12
What's Your Niche?

*I*t had been more than two years since I had received my last paycheck as a philosophy teacher. During that time I had been to seminary in Philadelphia, got married, and come back to Lincoln. Elizabeth had been working as a secretary for Animal Control for more than a year, and I was still unemployed. For some time I had been applying for jobs haphazardly—a teaching job here and there, a few pastorates, a job with the telephone company, one with a local aviation firm, and some others that have long since faded from my memory. I had even taken the postal service exam.

One Sunday after church, our pastor suggested that I study to get licensed in our denomination. "Doug," he said, "we're going to have several pulpits open up. You might be called to one of them. That will give you some experience in the ministry. This will increase your chances of teaching in seminary some day."

The next day I organized my material—my books, my lecture notes, my Greek and Hebrew flash cards—and began studying. No one was more eager for a job than I was. I was willing to take *anything* that came along. The thought of going into the pastorate really excited me. Yes, I would have preferred another job teaching philosophy. But being a pastor would surely be more up my alley than being a postal clerk—or so I thought.

Six years later I left the pastorate. During my years as a minister, I found myself waiting for the day I could do something else for a living. I enjoyed preaching and teaching, but that was about it. I wasn't much for working with youth or for counseling. Granted, I had had a very difficult congregation. But I also was a poor comforter and felt awkward chit-chatting during pastoral visits. I had chosen the wrong career.

There's a difference between getting a job and getting the right job. When someone is in an employment crisis—whether he's lost his job or is suffering from job burnout—he's tempted to take the first job that comes along. That is understandable. In the long term, however, it may be disastrous.

The goal for the person who is experiencing a job crisis is to *transcend* that crisis. However, transcending it involves more than getting another job. It involves finding a job you can love—or at least finding a job you can like a lot.

The purpose of this chapter is to help you to evaluate yourself. You need to determine what your talents are, what you enjoy doing, and how important job and financial security are to you. You need to ask yourself what sort of job you can envision yourself being happy in the rest of your life.

At times, of course, we will accept a full-time position that we know cannot give us happiness. Such employment is OK on a temporary basis, as we look for a better-suited position at that firm or somewhere else. Eventually we must find the job we can truly commit to in the long term.

The five questions that follow concerning your talents, job enjoyment, job security, financial security, and long-term staisfaction can help you determine whether the next job that comes up can be the permanent one you need. Answer each question honestly. If you don't, you may get stuck in a job you hate. And before long, you'll be in the midst of another job crisis.

YOUR TALENTS

First, what are your talents? Mr. McNamee was my English teacher when I was a sophomore in high school. He used to entertain us with many funny stories. One day he described his adventures while riding on trains. To pass the time, he would sit in the club car and strike up conversations with people. When the conversation turned to work, he never told them that he was an English teacher. (As he explained, he hated the inevitable comment, "Oh, now I'll have to watch my grammar.") So he would pass himself off as something else—world-famous organist E. Power Biggs, a corporate lawyer, or an accountant.

One day he told a rather husky man that he was a bricklayer. It so happened that this other man was also a bricklayer. When he found this out, Mr. McNamee quickly excused himself and took his five-foot-five-inch, 120-pound frame and headed for another part of the car.

As he told this story, the class roared with laughter. The thought of Mr. McNamee working as a bricklayer was hilarious. For Mr. McNamee, that job was clearly a poor fit.

Mr. McNamee's class was one of the few in which I paid close attention. In most other classes I daydreamed—more often than not about being a major league baseball player. I had absolutely no athletic ability and never even had the courage to try out for my high school team. But in my reverie all was different. I was coordinated, strong, could hit a ball out of any ballpark in the land, and possessed a great arm.

Mr. McNamee was an excellent English teacher. (I learned more about writing from him than from anyone else.) He may have made a decent accountant or lawyer, though we'll never know. But had he chosen to be a bricklayer, the results would have been disastrous.

There is a bit of Walter Mitty in all of us. We dream of being things we know we cannot be and have no serious intention of becoming. We know that if we're five feet five inches tall and weigh 120 pounds, we're never going to be a bricklayer. We know that not being good enough to try out for the high school team precludes future stardom as a professional baseball player. Our dreams are simply harmless forms of escape.

However, sometimes the mismatch isn't so obvious. We don't know exactly what our talents are or what skills a particular job or career requires. We get into something that doesn't quite match our talents, that requires skills we don't possess, or that fails to tap some of our strongest resources. We become frustrated and begin to hate our job. We may even lose it because of incompetence or indifference.

One of your goals, then, as you look for another job, is to find one that requires and uses *your* talents. To do this, you must do three things.

First, you have to determine what talents you possess. A good way to do this is by taking a talent-assessment test. These tests are widely available. (A variety of tests may be found in the books I have listed at the end of chapter 5.)

Next, you must find out what sorts of jobs require your particular set of talents. Your local library contains many reference works describing a wide variety of jobs. Start with the *Dictionary of Occupational Titles*, which is published by the United States Department of Labor and updated regularly.[6] This work gives a complete listing of all types of jobs available in the United States. These jobs are grouped by occupational category. You may be able to find out even more about the jobs that initially attract you by observing them firsthand or talking to people who do them.

Finally, you have to locate jobs that are presently available in your area of interest. If they are too far afield from anything you've done to date, you need to determine whether you possess transferable skills or whether you will need further training. (Chapter 4, and the books listed at the end of that chapter, will aid you in your job search at this point.)

The primary purpose of this chapter is not to provide an in-depth talent-assessment examination; however, you should consider the following questions to understand your abilities. As you answer these seven questions, you will begin to have a better perception of your talents.

1. *What sorts of hobbies and activities do you enjoy?* Make a list of the things you like to do. Include in this list things you enjoyed doing in the past but no longer engage in. Be as broad as possible. Don't just list your official "hobbies," but note your community, church, and school activities as well. My list includes baking, cooking, playing the piano and violin, model railroading, long-distance running, playing and watching baseball and basketball, gathering statistics, doing cost-analyses and comparisons, writing, teaching Bible studies and Sunday school, public speaking, and gardening. Yours might include such activities as painting, needlework, doing crossword puzzles, repairing appliances, singing, horseback riding, baby-sitting, entertaining guests, being active in environmental groups, and taking part in fund-raising activities.

Look over your list. You should be able to tell quite a bit about yourself. For instance, as I go over my list, I can see that, while I enjoy participating in certain group activities (such as baseball and basketball), I am not much of a "group" person. Many of my activities (e.g., gardening, baking, doing cost-analyses, running) I can do by myself. For those that require another person or persons, I don't have to relate *directly* to that person but can relate through an impersonal medium (e.g., the rules of a game) or through a fairly rigid structure (e.g., as teacher to students).

I tend to be musical and cerebral but not very mechanical. Model railroading is the only item on my list that requires significant mechanical skills. Even here, I generally buy already-built cars and ready-made tracks. My purpose in constructing a layout is simply to get it operative as quickly as possible, so I can start doing what I really enjoy—running the trains around the layout.

I enjoy detail work and analyzing data. I like to see tangible results from my efforts (e.g., a loaf of bread, a good crop of tomatoes, a tasty meal). And I am achievement-oriented.

This simple exercise tells me a lot about the sorts of jobs for which I might be suited. I wouldn't want to be an appliance repairman or an electrician. I doubt that I would be a very good family counselor. I would hate being a salesman. On the other hand, I might like a job where part of my duties were as a motivational speaker. (Here my contact with others would involve a clearly defined authority relationship.) I would probably make a very good accountant and an even better actuary.

2. *How do you best communicate with others?* Perhaps you think you don't communicate very well. You do. You may not communicate well through speaking or writing, but these are only two forms of communication. You can also communicate through music and art. You can even use your body to communicate.

These forms of communication can be broken down further. Teaching, public speaking, giving orders, and conversing are different forms of speaking, and they all require different skills. Surprising as it may seem, an excellent public speaker may be an indifferent teacher—and vice versa. Some of the best orators I have known have been almost incapable of carrying on a one-on-one conversation. Many wonderful conversationalists become incompetent once they get behind a teacher's lectern.

Writing isn't a monolithic entity, either. I wrote my last poem in high school, and I hope I never have to write another. Some people can write wonderful personal letters but can't organize a written report. The style of writing appropriate for an insurance policy would prove deadly if applied to a popular magazine article.

Before you consider a particular job, you need to determine what kinds of communication skills it requires. Some positions will require teaching others. In some you may write an occasional report and summarize your day's activities. You may have to speak to subordinates or draw illustrations.

All jobs require you to communicate. It's extremely important for you to recognize your strengths and weaknesses in the area of communication.

3. *What sort of physical skills do you possess?* The only things that stood between me and a major league baseball career were my lack of physical coordination, lack of speed, and lack of good eye-hand coordination. Other than that, I possessed all the tools necessary. Of course, what I just noted are the three physical skills most crucial to being a good ball-

player. My lack of them is probably the reason I didn't even play Little League ball, much less major league ball.

On the other hand, I possess a kind of manual dexterity that has allowed me, through practice, to be able to type one hundred-plus words per minute. This particular form of dexterity, however, does not automatically carry over to certain forms of precision work that must be done with the hands. I am a total klutz when it comes to constructing small-scale models. And although I've never tried it, I doubt that I would be a very good brain surgeon.

There are many different types of physical skills, and different jobs require or emphasize one type or another. Some jobs, such as certain types of construction work, require brute strength. Other construction work (such as roofing) emphasizes overall body coordination more than strength. A worker laying railroad track needs a combination of stamina and strength. A singer will be more efficient if she has high lung capacity even before she begins breathing exercises to enhance that capacity.

Possessing a particular physical skill is more important for some jobs than for others. But all jobs require you to do *something* with your body. Before you take a job, you should determine whether it will place physical demands upon you that you cannot meet.

4. *What sort of creative and analytic skills do you possess?* I keep the family checkbook and determine our budget. I keep all the records for our sports card business. When I thought about selling cleaning products, I spent many hours contentedly making cost-analyses. On the other hand, ask me to figure out how to put together a simple toy, and I am at a complete loss. Even with explicit instructions, I barely manage. Electrical circuitry is a mystery to me, and I have never figured out how an internal combustion engine works, despite having studied the matter on several occasions.

I'm a good baker and a decent cook, and I like to make my own creations. Although I know many people who are much better musicians overall, I feel I'm pretty good at composing my own tunes. However, when it comes to painting or handicrafts, not only are my efforts utter disasters, but I lose interest after about five minutes. I'm not much good at constructing diagrams, other than maps.

As with your physical skills, you need to determine your creative and analytical strengths and weaknesses. The job you choose must play into your strengths and avoid your weaknesses.

5. *What sort of people skills do you possess?* As I look back on my attempt to sell cleaning products the summer after I was married, I wonder how I even got out of bed much less into the car to make cold calls two weeks in a row. I am not a salesman. I never will be. This is one

Accountant or Librarian?

Your creative and analytical skills are just as varied as are your physical skills. For most jobs, knowing which ones you possess is even more important than knowing your physical capacities and limitations.

If you are not good at calculating, you probably will not make a very good accountant. If you don't reason from premises to conclusion, being a lawyer might not be your cup of tea. If you can't see cause and effect in the physical world, you probably won't be much of a mechanic or electrician.

Clearly, recognizing your creative and analytical strengths is an important step in finding a job that will satisfy you for the long term. If you cannot do calculations well but love to sort and classify, you might make a good librarian.

Consider these perfect matches: If you're constantly coming up with new theories about how things operate, you could be an ideal scientist or inventor. If you keep spotting other people's typos and grammatical mistakes, you might be a good proofreader or editor. No job will be perfect in all areas, but if your creative or analytical skills are being met, the chances of your long-term satisfaction are high.

"people skill" I obviously don't possess. This also limited my attempts at pastoral counseling.

Selling and counseling are only two of many people skills. Although no one possesses all the social skills for effective interaction with people, everyone has some of them. Here are a few of the more important: managing others, tutoring, instructing, serving, supporting people in need, evaluating others, motivating, negotiating, comforting, and convincing.

Although jobs require some people skills, some require more than others. Think of the diverse skills a supervisor must possess. He or she must be able to manage others, evaluate their performances, motivate them, instruct them, negotiate disputes, and possibly even counsel and comfort. A pastor needs most of these skills and others as well—such as convincing others and supporting them in their time of need.

A technical writer, on the other hand, may need few interpersonal skills. Even so, he will have to come into contact with others when he gathers information. He will need to be civil enough to make people favorably disposed to communicating the information he needs.

6. *Are you more comfortable meeting new people or do you prefer being alone?* Some jobs require you to continually meet new people. Many salesmen, for example, find that they must contact and establish rapport with new people almost daily. Consultants may also find themselves in this position. Other jobs demand that you relate well to people with whom you are already acquainted. Most people who work in offices do not have to meet new people on a regular basis. However, they do have to relate well to their coworkers.

Some jobs require you to spend long hours alone. A typist (as opposed to a secretary), a statistician, and a forest ranger may all spend most of their working hours by themselves. Many people who run home-based businesses or who are telecommuters are also in this situation.

You should determine the relational setting in which you feel most comfortable and then find a job that puts you in this setting. Unless you enjoy meeting new people and establishing new relationships on a regular basis, you will soon dislike a job that requires you to do this. Conversely, only if you enjoy spending most of your time alone will you thrive in a work environment that keeps you isolated from others. Make sure you know your own relational tendencies before you accept your next job.

7. *Are you a self-motivated person?* When you work for someone else, you're usually told what to do. If you get your assigned tasks done and do them well, your boss will be pleased. More often than not, you'll be kept on the job and will get regular salary increases. Many people thrive in this environment. The rules of the game are clear. They know just what is expected of them. And that's just the way they want it.

Not all jobs are like this. The self-employed person, of course, doesn't have someone else to tell him what to do. He must motivate himself to action. Similarly, certain jobs within a corporation contain a great deal of flexibility. The persons who fill these positions need to motivate themselves. They must create their own tasks and their own schedules. If you are a self-motivated person, you may be ideally suited for this sort of position.

However, if you aren't, you will find this sort of flexibility extremely frustrating, possibly even debilitating. You may arrive at work each day wondering what to do, not sure which tasks should have priority. Some days you will be unable to motivate yourself to start working.

Such people need and enjoy set tasks in a regulated environment; they find satisfaction in completing projects in a set time frame. In an unstructured setting with much independence, they will be frustrated.

On the other hand, if you are a self-motivated person, the sort of job where you're told exactly what to do would be equally frustrating. You would continually see ways in which you could improve upon the rules set by your supervisor. You may even start doing things by your own rules.

And, though you may get away with this for a while, eventually, you will come into conflict with your boss. If the conflict is severe enough, you may be fired.

Once you've conducted your talent assessment, you've taken the first crucial step to finding the right job. But it's just the first step. You still need to answer four more questions.

ENJOYING THE JOB

During the six years I was in the pastorate, I preached almost every Sunday. I was a talented public speaker. However, I soon discovered that I didn't enjoy preaching nearly as much as lecturing philosophy classes years earlier. For that matter, I didn't enjoy preaching as much as teaching adult Sunday school classes. Even after six years behind the pulpit, I still felt a certain nervousness when I began my sermon. I probably preached and taught equally well, but I enjoyed the second task much more than the first.

As you search for the right job, you need to consider not only your talents but what you enjoy doing. You may be a talented musician, but if you hate performing, you won't want to become a professional musician. You may be an extremely good baker, but if you don't like baking, there's no point in applying for a job at your local bakery.

The second question you should ask when considering a permanent, full-time job is: *Will I enjoy this job?* There are only two ways to determine whether you will like something. You can try it and see. Or you can look to past experience. Did you like it the last time you did it (or did something similar)?

Here's where your list of enjoyable hobbies and activities can help you. If several of your past activities are similar to what you will be doing in a job you've applied for, there's a good chance you will like the job. This is especially true if these activities were those that you found especially enjoyable or excelled at. However, if you find nothing on this list that even remotely corresponds to what you will be doing, the chances are strong that eventually you will despise the job.

JOB SECURITY

Rick Filkin was manager of the shipping department at General Data Corporation. He had worked for General Data for eighteen years and was well liked by both his superiors and his subordinates. In addition, General Data was rock solid. Rick's job was secure. There was only one problem— he was bored stiff with what he was doing.

Rick had a long-standing interest in gourmet cooking, and for some time he had wanted to go into the restaurant business. To this end, he had taken a number of evening courses in food management at the local community college. When his good friend, Bill Curry, decided to open a second restaurant, he asked Rick whether he would consider being its manager. Curry's Steak and Seafood had been open for five years and had done reasonably well. But like many restaurants, it faced tough competition. There was no guarantee that this first restaurant would last, much less the second.

Rick faced a dilemma. He knew he would enjoy managing Curry's Seaside, Bill's proposed name for his second restaurant. But he also knew that if he took this job, he might be out of work in another year. For some time, Rick struggled with his decision. In the end, he chose job security. He declined Bill's offer and decided to stay with General Data, at least for the time being. Six months after Curry's Seaside opened for business, it closed its doors. Rick had made the right decision.

The third question in considering a full-time job is: *How important is job security for me?* Evaluate the security of the prospective job and how important that security is to you. In the best of all possible job worlds, the job for which you are best suited is also the one that is most secure. But in the real world, it seldom works that way. You may have to face the decision of *what's more important—job security or job contentment.* If job security is extremely important for you, it may actually become an important factor in your overall job contentment. You may willingly stick out an otherwise unappealing job because "at least it's secure."

If you are presently in an employment crisis, you must consider the importance you place in a job's security. Would you leave a boring but secure job for an exciting one that's insecure? If you are presently unemployed, are you going to jump at the first job that promises security, or will you hold out for one you'll really enjoy, even if it's less secure? (See "A Secure Job" for ways you can measure your need for job security.)

FINANCIAL SECURITY

Like job security, financial security is also important. For some people, it's all-important. The fourth question is: *How will the new position affect your financial security, and how important to you is financial security?*

Ever since her husband had become partially paralyzed in an automobile accident twelve years earlier, Brenda Honeck had supported him and their two children by working as a computer programmer at Northwest Casualty Insurance Company. Her position was well-paying and se-

A Secure Job

For many people job security is more important than job contentment. For some, job security is essential for feeling contented about a job. To help you determine the importance of job security, consider these three questions:

1. *Are you a risk-taker?* If you are, security may not be an important factor. On the other hand, if you've always preferred the tried and predictable, security may be an overriding consideration in your decision.
2. *What other people will be affected if you lose your job?* Security may be a much more important consideration for a family man than for a single individual. As Rick Filkin told Bill Curry, "If I were single, I wouldn't hesitate managing Seaside [restaurant] for a moment. But with two kids in high school, we've got to have some money when they go to college." Rick chose to forego a promising job in a new field because of its uncertain future.
3. *How insecure is your potential situation?* Compare the security of your present (or last) position with the security of the potential new job. If the difference isn't all that great, you will probably be more likely to consider a change. If you're contemplating a pie-in-the-sky possibility, you may be extremely hesitant to take it. A year and a half after Rick Filkin turned down Bill Curry, he was offered the position of assistant food manager at the local Hilton hotel. He knew that this position was nearly as stable as his present job. So he handed in his resignation to General Data and went to work at the Hilton.

cure. However, like Rick Filkin, she was bored with her work. After taking a talent-assessment test and talking over the results with a career counselor, Brenda decided to become a journalist. She had had several journalism courses in college. In the years since graduation, she had continued to write. She had edited the in-house newsletter for Northwest Casualty and had written much of its copy. She had even written a short-lived column on gardening for a local weekly. When a job as a reporter on the *American News* opened up, Brenda applied and was offered the job.

Like Rick, Brenda faced a dilemma. But unlike Rick's, which involved job security, Brenda's dilemma involved money. Brenda knew that if she proved herself, she would have a secure job on the newspaper staff. But she also knew that she would earn only two-thirds of what she was making at Northwest Casualty. She struggled with her decision. Money was important, but the children were nearly grown, and therefore it was less a consideration than it would have been several years earlier. On the other hand, her desire for job satisfaction was overwhelming. Brenda quit her job and went to work on the newspaper.

Jack Bowman faced a different sort of financial dilemma. Years earlier, he had been a salesman for Midland Hardware Supply Company. He had really enjoyed this work. However, after getting married, he decided to "settle down." For him, that meant finding a steady job working at Hammerstein Lumber Company. After several years, Jack was making enough to support his family in a comfortable fashion. But Jack soon developed a desire to go back on the road and sell. He still had several contacts at Midland, and from them he learned that Midland really wanted him back on its sales force. He knew that the potential for financial gain was much greater as a salesman. At the same time, he knew that he would be working entirely on commission and that therefore the financial risk was great. After deliberating for some time, Jack decided the risk was worth it and cast his lot with Midland.

Brenda and Jack both wanted a more fulfilling job. They both had to give up a position in which they had financial security to get the job they wanted. Brenda's problem was that she knew that she would be earning much less in her new job. Jack's was that he didn't know what he would earn. If everything went right, he would be financially successful. If everything went wrong, he would be financially ruined.

Financial insecurity takes many forms. These are two of the most common. Whenever a new job involves financial insecurity, you must determine how important financial security is for you. The factors involved are similar to those for job security. You need to decide (1) whether you are willing to take risks, (2) how your decision will affect other people, particularly members of your family, and (3) how much more insecure your new financial position will be. A slight cut in salary is a small price to pay for overall job satisfaction. However, if your new job cuts your earnings in half, you might want to reconsider.

LOOKING TO THE LONG TERM

Let's assume that you've made your talent assessment. You know what you want to do. You've been offered a job that will allow you to do it.

You've examined the financial risks and the question of job security. You decide that these risks aren't any greater than they are now; or, if they are, they are worth taking. You are now ready to accept your new job.

You need to ask yourself one more question. *Can I envision being happy in this job the rest of my working life?*

Notice that I didn't ask whether you think this is the perfect job. Believe me, it's not. If you think it's perfect, you will be sorely disappointed. Your new job will have its drawbacks. Every job does.

In this respect, jobs are like spouses—although I'm not suggesting that you become married to your job the way you are to your spouse. Your spouse isn't perfect. No human being is perfect. Nevertheless, your spouse can be the very best spouse *for you.* And you can love your spouse wholeheartedly—in spite of his or her imperfections.

The same goes for your job. You will not find the perfect job, but you might find the best job for you. If you get the best job for you, it will be one that you can love. And just as two imperfect individuals can be happy with their marriage throughout its duration, so too you can have a job in which you can be happy the rest of your working life.

That's why it's very important to ask yourself the above question. If you think you will lose interest in your job in a year or two, if even now you see severe limitations and drawbacks, if you are trading one lousy situation for another, then don't take this job. Hold out for one in which you think you can be happy. If you do, you'll find a job you can love. At last, you will find your niche.

13
A Business Opportunity for You

For years I've had a flexible schedule that has allowed me to do some or all of my work at home. As a philosophy teacher, I didn't have to go to campus unless I had a class, a faculty meeting, or appointments with students. When I was a pastor, I did much of my studying and sermon preparation in my office at home. The rest of my adult life, I've been either unemployed or self-employed.

For nearly two decades, I've had the flexibility to shop for groceries during midday on weekdays. I like shopping then because the stores aren't crowded. During this time, I've noticed a subtle but almost continuous increase in the number of men who shop during these hours. Twelve years ago I could have assumed that any of the men I saw in the stores were either unemployed or worked second or third shift at one of the local factories. The sheer number of men today forces me to reach a different conclusion. Some or most of them are self-employed and probably are working at home.

I see them at the playground as well, caring for their young children. While most of the adults are still women, each summer a few more men join their ranks. Clearly, a shift is taking place in the work force, a shift toward self-employment and working at home.

This shift is borne out by statistics. As of 1990, there were approximately 27 million full-time or part-time home-based businesses.[7] It is estimated that by 1995 there will be 20.7 million full-time home-based businesses alone.[8] The number of part-time businesses will also increase significantly. These figures do not include the increasingly large number of "telecommuters"—people who work at home but who are employed by someone else. Obviously, we are on the tip of an iceberg.

---

he number and variety of goods and services marketed from the home are enormous, and the possibilities are endless.

These home-based businesses range from consulting firms, accounting services, and word processing services to cookie and candy making, woodworking, and doll making. They include all sorts of mail-order enterprises, from baseball cards to sunflower seeds. Some involve small retail shops operated in the den of a house or an out-building. Others manufacture goods on the kitchen table or at a small workbench in the basement. The number and variety of goods and services marketed from the home are enormous, and the possibilities are endless.

What sorts of people work from home? All sorts. Some are unemployed men and women trying to make a new life for themselves. Others are building up a business, hoping for the day when they will be able to leave a distasteful job. Some are housewives making a little bit of extra money for the family. Others are successful professional men and women who prefer to offer their services and expertise on their own rather than through an employer. Some are retired or semiretired individuals wanting to keep busy. Others are men and women in their late teens or early twenties who hope they never have to enter the work force. Some are risk-takers. Others aren't. The one thing they all have in common is that they are all entrepreneurs.

Is starting a home-based business for you? We will answer that question in this chapter. However, before we do, we need to make some distinctions.

Home workers fall into two categories—those who are self-employed and those who are employed by someone else. Because of several important differences in the way the two groups must file their taxes, the Internal Revenue Service has a set of criteria to determine whether a home worker is self-employed. If you're interested in this, you may consult the works listed at the end of the chapter. For our purposes, a self-employed home worker is one who runs his own business or contracts out his services to several individuals or firms. Generally speaking, he is responsible for obtaining his own life and health insurance and for paying the full share of his Social Security tax.

A home worker who is employed by someone else is sometimes called a *telecommuter.* This is because his "commute" to his employer's office is typically by telephone or some other form of telecommunication—such as a fax machine or computer terminal and modem. Some telecommuters work almost entirely at home. Others arrange their schedules to go into the central office one or two days a week. Typically, a telecommuter works for one employer. He works at home for his employer's convenience (or for mutual convenience). Often, his equipment (such as his computer and modem) is supplied by his employer. He receives a salary set by his employer. He is eligible for group health and life insurance. And his employer pays half his Social Security tax.

Most of what we will be discussing in this chapter is intended for home workers who are *not* telecommuters. However, some of the problems that we will discuss are faced by *all* home workers, including telecommuters. If you are presently a telecommuter or thinking of becoming one, you should pay careful attention to these points.

Many of the problems facing the home-based business are common to all self-employment ventures, including the self-employed who rent offices or small shops away from home. So, even if your goal is to operate from a store front or an office outside your home, much of what we will discuss in this chapter is for you.

THE RIGHT ATTITUDE

Book after book has been written on the key to succeeding as a self-employed person. Generally, these books focus on one particular aspect

of the self-employment venture—marketing, pricing, advertising, customer relations, location, and so on. All these aspects are important. But
there's something even more important. Before we discuss any of the specifics of how to start and run your own business, we need to single this
out. This most important ingredient can be captured in one simple word—
attitude.

*Y ou need to enter your business
venture with the right attitude
if you want to succeed. The
right attitude contains three ingredients: trust, patience, and hope.*

If you want to succeed, you need to enter your business venture with
the right attitude. The right attitude contains three ingredients.

First, there is *trust.* You must trust in God, trust that He is in control of
your venture, and that whether you succeed or fail, He will see you
through.

Next comes *patience.* You need to realize that you will not succeed
overnight. Most businesses don't take off immediately. In fact, most make
very little money in the first six months to two years. If you want the cash
to start flowing in today, you're in the wrong enterprise. However, the biblical principle "Who despises the day of small things?" (Zechariah 4:10)
applies here. I've adopted this as my motto for my own home-based ventures: *Bit by bit, little by little.* (See Isaiah 28:10, KJV.) Another way to put
this is: *Two steps forward, one step back.* As long as I'm taking more steps
forward than I am backward, I know I'm making progress. God won't work
a miracle with my business overnight. But as I look back over a month, a
quarter, a year, I can see that He has allowed me to move ahead. That is
all I can ask for.

Finally comes *hope.* If you think you're going to fail, you will. If you
have hope that you'll succeed, you probably will. How can you maintain
hope, even when everything seems to be headed in reverse, even when
you haven't seen a penny coming in for a month, even when you don't
know where you'll get the money to order any more product? By trusting in
God. If you have that first ingredient, this third ingredient will follow. If you
don't, you'll eventually sink in the mire of despair.

PITFALLS

Having the right attitude is crucial. But you must also avoid certain pitfalls if your business is to succeed. Some of these are more critical than others, but any one of them can doom a venture.

Pitfall #1: Direct-Sales Organizations

Most books on starting your own business don't even bother to mention direct-sales organizations. Perhaps they think that the reader is smart enough to know that most people cannot make a full-time living in such organizations. I know. I've been in three direct-sales organizations in my life. Two I joined to buy their products at wholesale for my personal use without any intention of selling them on the retail market. I got into the other organization thinking I was going to make a wonderful living selling their products—a line of chemical products for the car, the home, and the farm. My entry fee was $2,500, of which $500 went for a motivational training session. The remaining $2,000 went for product. I sold about half of this over a period of several years, used some, and threw the rest away. I figure my net loss was somewhere in the neighborhood of $750—not a very good business venture.

What, exactly, is a direct-sales organization? While the details of their structure may vary, they operate somewhat as follows: A company will manufacture and seek to market a certain product or products (e.g., vitamins, cleaning products, beauty aids, fuel additives). Rather than distributing these products to wholesalers (who in turn pass them on to retailers), it recruits independent salesmen to be its distributors. Recruiting a national sales force can be costly and time-consuming. To avoid this, such companies encourage their initial sales force to recruit their own distributors and thereby develop their own sales force. The distributors on this next level are encouraged to recruit yet more distributors, and so on.

To give its distributors incentive to build up as large a sales force as possible, the company pays a bonus to those distributors whose sales force reaches a certain size. The bonus is typically a percentage of the total sales of the distributor's recruits in a given time period—usually a month. The size of that percentage is often determined by the complexity of the distributor's sales force.

Direct-sales organizations have hit upon an interesting way of distributing their products. When new distributors are recruited, then, it is often stressed that the real money comes through building up a sales force. However, in many instances, a city or even the entire county becomes saturated with salespeople.

But the new recruit doesn't realize this at first. If he or she attends one of the organization's motivational meetings (and these organizations have several national and regional meetings each year), he sees several well-dressed, obviously well-heeled couples honored for their sales efforts. The new distributor is soon convinced that in a matter of months, a year at the most, he will be just like them. In his initial enthusiasm, he feverishly tries to recruit other distributors. He may even try to sell some product at the suggested retail price. (This price tends to be high, both to pay bonuses to the distributors and to cover the higher costs of manufacturing smaller quantities than are those of the commercial competitors.) He soon finds that few who are not already in the organization share his enthusiasm.

If people join a direct-marketing organization simply to pass the time, to meet new people, or to earn part-time money, their experience will probably meet their expectations. However, unemployed people often get involved. So do people who are fed up with their current job. A person going through a job crisis needs to do something constructive to help him transcend that crisis. He doesn't need a detour down the direct-sales organization road.

If you're thinking of starting your own business, stay clear of direct-sales organizations. For every person who succeeds, hundreds fail. Take the organization in which I was involved. Though my group manager later became a successful roofing contractor, he failed in his direct-sales venture. My area manager went bankrupt.

Pitfall #2: Bad Ideas

If you're going to have a home business, you need an idea. Some ideas are good. Some are bad. If you have a bad idea, your business won't succeed, no matter how good your advertising, no matter how fair your price, and no matter how motivated you are.

Ideas can fail for any number of reasons. For instance, the market for your product or service may be glutted. Suppose you decide you want to become a chimney sweep. You invest in the necessary equipment, advertise your services, and wait for your phone to start ringing. It never does. After a while, you get a bit of business, but not enough to generate significant income. Later you contact the other chimney sweeps in town. You learn that they have barely enough business to keep going. Obviously, the market is glutted. It will remain that way unless a significant number of new houses with fireplaces are constructed.

Your home business may be unable to produce a product capable of competing with those already on the market. Or your product or service may fail to fill a felt need that people have. As a college student, Jason Cole had a friend who would go to the local fast-food outlets and pick up food late at night for the fellows in the dorms and frat houses. He charged a small fee and many students, too busy to go themselves or without transportation, gladly paid Jason's friend. The friend did quite a business meeting their demand. Jason remembered this service, and after he graduated, he decided to set up a similar service in the middle-class neighborhood into which he had moved. He had flyers printed up, and distributed them door to door. Jason had no takers. He had failed to realize that families are different from college students. Families typically make eating fast food into a "family outing." Moreover, they have their own transportation. Finally, they are seldom so busy that they don't have time to run to the fast-food establishment themselves. The people in Jason's neighborhood just didn't perceive a need for his services.

You can go a long way toward weeding out your bad ideas beforehand. Check to see if anyone else is doing what you're thinking of doing. If they aren't, why not? Is it because no one needs your product or service? Or is it because there's a big gap waiting to be filled? If others are already offering what you have to offer, is the market still wide open or is it glutted? (Check to see how others are faring. Do they have more work than they can handle or are they scrambling to find work?)

Will your product or service be cost-competitive or not? Determine what you'll have to charge to make an acceptable profit. See what your competitors are charging. Make your decision on the basis of this. For some products or services, you may actually have an advantage. For others (particularly those that require significant investment in equipment), you may not.

Ask your friends what they think. Would they buy your product or use your service? Can they think of others who would? If none of your friends show much enthusiasm for your venture, you can be pretty sure you've hit on a bad idea.

These are just a few suggestions for weeding out your bad ideas. Consult the books listed at the end of this chapter for more detailed advice.

Pitfall #3: Debt

A home-based business requires capital. Unless you have a considerable amount of money saved up, you will be tempted to go into debt to finance your business. Even if you start with your savings, you'll be tempted to take out a loan when you expand your business.

The temptation will be greater than you think. When I first started my sports card business, I used savings to build up my inventory. I was proud that I didn't have to take out a loan. Elizabeth and I were agreed that we would never go into debt to finance this business. However, after I had been working the business for a little over a year, I had the chance to pick up a considerable amount of product that I was sure I could sell within a couple of months at a tremendous profit. The only way I could get all I wanted was to take out a loan. I was sorely tempted to do this. But after Elizabeth and I prayed about it, we decided to forego the loan and buy a smaller amount of the product in question. After all, we had agreed never to go into debt. As it turned out, I would have been able to sell the extra product and make an even greater profit than I did. But I don't regret our decision. Deficit financing is simply not worth it.

---

*D*eficit financing is simply not worth it. Debt can be damaging . . .

Debt can be damaging, particularly if you are just starting a business. You've probably read the horror statistics. Some 80 percent of businesses fail within two years of start-up. But behind that statistic is that one small word—*debt*. Don't get me wrong. Some businesses succeed marvelously despite deficit financing. And some businesses fail for reasons that have nothing to do with debt. But the surest way to dig yourself into a hole you can't escape is to take out a loan to start your business.

Remember, businesses take time to build up. Many of them don't turn a profit in the first six months to two years. There's a reason for this. You need to establish a customer base, and you need to advertise to do this. In addition, if you are selling a product, you need to build up your inventory. Those first several months you won't have much cash inflow. What you have you will want to put back into advertising and inventory. If you are saddled with a loan payment of several hundred dollars or more per month, you may not have money to do this. You may not even have enough cash flow to make your payments on the loan.

Not going into debt means that you may have to start small and build up your business bit by bit, little by little. (Remember my motto.) But doing it this way is worth it. Your chances of long-term success are greatly increased.

Pitfall #4: Lack of Motivation

If you're a self-employed person, particularly if you work at home, you will have to motivate yourself every single morning. You don't have a time-clock to punch. You don't have a boss looking over your shoulder. You may not have a specific set of tasks you need to accomplish. The easiest thing in the world is to put off your work. Before you know it, the day is spent, and you've done nothing.

Two things can be helpful in overcoming this daily motivational problem. First, wake up at the same time every morning and go through a certain routine. For me, this means getting dressed, doing calisthenics, running three to six miles, showering and shaving, reading my Bible, praying, eating breakfast, and writing in my journal. I usually start and finish each of these at nearly the same time each day.

You may not find this sort of schedule to your liking. After all, one of the advantages of working at home is that you have flexibility as to when you work and what you do. The important thing, though, isn't getting up at the same time every morning. It's establishing a certain routine (at whatever time of the day you do it) so that you can get in the mood for work.

Second, set aside a definite number of hours each day to devote to your work. Decide that you will spend, say, six hours working your job and abide by your decision. Even if you don't have a whole lot to do on a particular day, spend some time performing a task related to your job.

I have little trouble getting motivated for my sports card business. This particular business requires simply that I be around the house to take telephone orders, deal with in-person customers, place orders with manufacturers, write and mail a monthly newsletter, and keep the books. I know that as long as I handle these tasks, I've done my work. I don't have to put in a certain number of hours each day.

I do have trouble motivating myself to write. However, I know that if I don't *start* writing, I will not write at all. So each day I resolve to spend a certain number of hours working on a writing or editing project. If I have no assignments at all, either I do research on some topic in which I'm interested or I write query letters to magazine editors suggesting articles I would like to write. If I have absolutely nothing else to do, I'll send out reprints of articles I have published in the hope that some other magazine will pick them up. No matter what, I work. That's the important thing.

Pitfall #5: Family Distractions

Unless you're single, you will find yourself distracted by your family. Even if you are single, you may have friends who pop over for a visit and who simply don't understand that people who work at home must *work* at home. Dealing with these distractions is extremely important.

You shouldn't ignore your family. At the same time, they must be made to realize that you cannot work well with constant interruptions. Set aside a specific area of the house for work. Ideally, this should be a

How to Deal with Discouragement

Perhaps the deepest depression of Pitfall #4 is the feeling of discouragement. Nothing contributes to a lack of motivation like discouragement. What do you do when the weeks pass without a sale or productive contact in your home business? Many promising home business fail simply because the entrepeneur is overwhelmed by discouragement.

Remember, a home business does not progress along a smooth and gradually ascending plane. It's a series of ups and downs, peaks and valleys. When discouragement comes—and it will— you must not lose your motivation.

Here are some ways to lift your spirits and gain some inspiration for the task ahead. At the same time, you will have a truer perspective of your options.

1. Take a day off for play and perspective. Play with your kids. Watch a baseball game. Read a fun book.
2. Read a book on how to succeed in a home business. Listen to a motivational tape.
3. Spend extra time in prayer or Bible reading.
4. Go out to dinner with the family. One day will not destroy the family budget.

separate room. This area should be off-limits to your family during your work hours.

Obviously you shouldn't take this to extremes. If your little boy cuts his hand, you shouldn't keep working while he cries in pain and bleeds profusely all over your good couch. But you should have times that, barring such emergencies, you can count on as being uninterrupted work periods.

If your work requires intense concentration and you need quiet, your family should be sensitive to this need. You should either locate your work area some distance from the television and play areas or make sure that family members know that they must be relatively quiet while you are working.

If you need to talk to clients, you may have to set certain rules of conduct for your family. For instance, you may want to insist that your family members do not enter your office unless they are decently dressed.

You may find a stereo blaring in the background inappropriate for such conferences. If so, make this clear to your family as well.

A SMOOTH START

Though you must be aware of the five pitfalls mentioned above, there are many ways you can assure an at-home business a healthy start. We will look at seven key elements to a smooth start: (1) the right place, (2) regard for city regulations, (3) proper records, (4) regard for tax regulations, (5) proper pricing, (6) the right advertising, and (7) a willingness to start.

The Right Place

Someone has wisely said that the three things that matter most in your business are "location, location, and location." This is almost as true for home businesses as for others. Some naturally gravitate to one area of the house or another. A cookie-making enterprise will be run out of the kitchen and a furniture-repair business will probably use the garage or basement workshop. Even if you run one of these, you probably will want a desk where you can keep your records, and you will have to decide where to locate it. For most home businesses, however, you will have the whole house to choose from. You should choose your work area with care.

One primary consideration is *privacy*. If you have a family or are living with other people, this is a crucial matter. If your work takes mental concentration, you should try to locate it in a separate room. If you don't have a spare room, at least locate your work area as far from family traffic as you can. You may consider investing in a room divider to partially isolate your work station. If you use a phone frequently in your business, make sure you have an extension in this room or work area.

If your business involves customers or clients coming into your home, easy *public access* is important. You need a space near an entrance where you can do business with your customers. Ideally, this should be a room right next to a side entrance, away from the living area of the house. Most home business people don't have this advantage. The next best thing is to locate your business space as near to the front or rear entrance as possible. It's important that your customers and clients do not have to go past bedrooms or through your kitchen while your family is eating. Make it so your guests don't feel as though they are intruding on your family's privacy.

Lighting in your office or work space should be adequate. Whether natural or artificial, proper lighting is essential if you do much paper work or frequently host customers or clients. Even if you don't have many clients, good lighting is important. It's better for your eyes. Moreover, working in semidarkness can be gloomy and depressing.

Finally, arrange your work space so that everything you need is readily *accessible*—records, telephone, computer, supplies, equipment, and so on. Once you get to your office or work station, you don't want to have to be running all over the house. Not only is this time-consuming, but you may find yourself distracted by family members, the television, or chores that need to be done.

Regard for City Regulations

Any time you run a business out of your house, you stand the risk of violating zoning regulations. Some municipalities have extremely rigid regulations that, if enforced, would effectively shut down a large percentage of home businesses.

Often these regulations aren't enforced unless someone complains. Still, you wouldn't want to take a chance. Other cities and towns are much more liberal. Check the regulations in your locality before you begin your enterprise. If technically you would be in violation of the law but you know you will be doing something that won't upset any of your neighbors, you may want to apply for a variance. This will allow you to legally operate your business.

It is very unlikely that you will be violating any zoning regulations if your business does not involve the making or repairing of any product, does not require you to meet customers or clients in your home, or does not involve receiving large shipments. A writer, a typist, a consultant, a lawyer, or an accountant is probably safe—if he or she deals with clients by phone or meets them outside the house. However, a bicycle or antiques repairman, or anyone with frequent customers, ought to check the community regulations. So should anyone wanting to operate a mail-order business.

If your business involves cooking or baking, you'll also need to check local health regulations. You may need a permit or have to meet certain sanitary standards. You may be subject to periodic checks. You may find out that you can't operate this sort of business at all. Check before you begin, and abide by all regulations. You may save yourself a lot of grief further down the road.

Proper Records

You need to keep complete records for at least two reasons. You need to know the financial health of your business. And the IRS wants to know about its health. If you don't keep good records, you will at best have a vague idea of how well the business is doing. Moreover, the tax man will be mighty upset. You may wind up paying a whole lot more than you would have if you had kept careful records.

I *f you don't keep good records, you will have a vague idea of how well the business is do-ing. . . . And the tax man will be mighty upset.*

The sort of records you must maintain will vary from business to business. At a minimum, you will need a record of all your receipts and expenses. Your expenses include the products you purchase, supplies, equipment, business-related telephone calls, advertising, business travel, and so forth. If you use part of your home exclusively for your business, you will need a record of your rent or the interest you pay on your mortgage, your real estate taxes, and your utilities. If you use an automobile or truck in your business, you'll want to keep a record of business mileage traveled, cost of gas, oil and repairs, tolls, and business-related parking expenses.

The above is only a general overview. To know more about record keeping, read the books I have listed at the end of this chapter. You may also meet with an accountant. He should be able to advise you on the exact records needed for your particular business. He may even be willing to show you how to keep your own books.

You may even want to retain the services of an accountant to do your books for you. I advise this only if your record keeping becomes extremely complicated or you feel you are totally incapable of working with figures. I believe that most people who run home businesses can keep their own books once they know how.

Regard for Tax Regulations

Once you start your home business you will have filed your last 1040A tax form. In fact, your return will, in all likelihood, be several pages thick and will include a variety of schedules and forms. It is up to you to know all the Internal Revenue Service regulations governing your business.

You can obtain this information from the IRS itself. Or you may consult any one of a number of books devoted to home businesses. (Several of the books listed at the end of this chapter contain this information.) Or you may consult an accountant or tax lawyer. Do what feels most comfortable to you.

Incidentally, a tax lawyer should be able to help you to decide whether or not to *incorporate*. There are many pros and cons to incorporating. The right decision will depend largely upon the financial situation in which you find yourself and the nature of your business. Many books on home businesses deal with this issue. However, my feeling is that you should consult a tax lawyer if you have *any* desire to incorporate. He will be able to look at your particular situation and determine whether incorporating will be to your advantage. Moreover, should you decide to incorporate, he will be able to draw up the necessary documents and file them with the appropriate agencies.

You will also need to be aware of state sales tax regulations. A freelance writer, editor, or a consultant will not need to collect state sales tax. However, those selling a product or offering other services may be required to pay. Check with your state department of revenue.

If your product or service is subject to state sales tax, you will need to obtain a sales tax collection permit. You will probably have to fill out a relatively simple form and pay a small filing fee. (It's to the advantage of departments of revenue to make the collection of sales tax as simple as possible.) You will then be able to collect sales tax, which you will be asked to remit to the state at regular intervals (monthly, quarterly, or annually).

Proper Pricing

Know the proper price for your goods or service. Obviously, if you charge too much, you will price yourself out of the market. However, it's just as dangerous to charge too little. There are two reasons for this.

Charging too little can create a sales resistance of its own. That is particularly true if you are offering goods or services for which there is an established price range. For instance, if everyone else in town is charging $4.00 per pound for homemade cookies and you charge $2.00, you immediately create the suspicion that "there must be something wrong with them." If accountants in your area are charging an average of $60 per hour and you charge $30, many people will think that "he can't be very good."

There's a true story about a man who made little metal toys in his basement workshop. They cost him almost nothing to make and he could produce a couple dozen per hour. He decided to rent space in a mall to sell them. He knew that he could make an acceptable profit selling them at 50 cents each. The first day he displayed his merchandise, many people stopped to look at his toys, but almost no one bought any. The second day he did an experiment. He raised the price to $1.00. By day's end, he had sold most of his stock. When he had his toys priced low, everybody thought they were junk. When he raised his price, people thought they were getting quality merchandise, and they bought accordingly.

A second reason to avoid charging too little is because doing so is an almost certain recipe for disaster. Not all your competitors are getting rich selling their merchandise or services. In all likelihood, the going rate represents what your competitors have found they need to charge to have a viable business. If your price is much below this rate, the profit will be so small that you will waste your time and energy.

Perhaps you think that by undercutting your competitors you will soon capture the lion's share of the market and that what you don't get in profit margin you can make up for in volume. It's certainly true that you'll make a lot more if you sell $100,000 in merchandise at a 10 percent markup than you will if you sell $1,000 at a 50 percent markup. But if you think your sales will jump drastically by offering lower prices, you've oversimplified the psychology of the buyer. People buy location, familiarity, service, and name-recognition as well as price. Moreover, as I've already indicated, too low a price will create buyer resistance. A lower price will not guarantee significantly greater volume.

The Right Advertising

Products and services don't sell themselves. You have to advertise. There are countless ways to advertise. Some are free or relatively inexpensive. Others cost a fortune.

If you don't want to spend a lot of money, consider advertising your product or service on a public-service bulletin board. Your advertisement can be as simple as a three-by-five card or a photocopied sheet of paper. Or you can stick one of your business cards on the board. (Many typists advertise their services this way.)

Another relatively inexpensive way to advertise is through the classifieds in your local newspaper. You can save money by advertising only on weekends, when more people will see your ad. If your town has a weekly shoppers' paper, check out its rates. They're usually reasonable, and you may be able to get a significant discount if you run your ad several weeks in a row.

If you want to advertise in your neighborhood, print up flyers and distribute them door to door. Your spouse and children can help you do this. This, too, is a relatively inexpensive way to make your service or product known.

If you want to market your service or product nationally, consider advertising in a national trade magazine or professional journal. You will pay more for this ad than for a classified in a local daily, but your exposure will be increased immeasurably.

---

*T*ry various forms of advertising. See which ones work for you. Continue with the ones that do; drop the ones that don't.

Another possibility is direct-mail marketing. This is not as straightforward as some other forms of advertising. You don't simply want to pick names from the phone book. You must mail your advertisements to people who are likely to buy your product. Thus, you need to generate a mailing list of potential customers. I've done this in my business by keeping a file of the names and addresses of all my local customers as well as those who have answered my national ads. As a result, I now have a mailing list of several hundred names. Because these people have bought from me before, I know that most of them are in the market for the type of products I have for sale. It has taken me a long time to build up this list. However, I have a much better mailing list than I would have had if I had simply bought one from another business or organization.

Direct mailings, of course, are expensive. You have to take into account not only your postage, but the cost of your envelopes and flyers. Moreover, you can expect no more than a one to two percent response rate to your mailings. You may even get less. (Because of the way I've developed my mailing list, I tend to get a much higher rate. But typically my response rate runs no higher than 10 percent.) Unless you can show that your profit from the sales that result is considerably higher than your costs, direct-mail advertising is not worth it.

There is no one right way to advertise. What works for one business may not work for another. What doesn't work today may work tomorrow. My advice is to try various forms of advertising. See which ones work for you. Continue with the ones that do; drop the ones that don't.

Evaluating the success of your advertising is important. In making your evaluation, however, don't just look at the initial response to your ad. Repeat business is equally important to consider. I have run ads where I have barely made enough to cover the cost of the ad. But some of these ads I consider to have been extremely successful. Why? Because I've picked up valued customers who have paid for the ad many times over.

One final word on advertising. One of the most important forms of advertising is *word-of-mouth advertising*. It can make or break your business. You may think you have no control over what others say about your business, but you do. That is why it's so important to give good, quick, reliable service and to make sure that you have a quality product to offer. If you run a lousy business, all your advertising is ultimately going to go for naught. If, on the other hand, you have a great product and reliable service, you're going to succeed. You will have the best advertising in the world—satisfied customers!

Ready To Go

Businesses fail for a variety of reasons. They are undercapitalized. They take on too much debt. They charge too much. They charge too little. They advertise too much. They don't advertise enough. They advertise in the wrong way. They fail to keep proper records. All these reasons contribute to the 80 percent failure rate of new businesses.

However, there's only one way for you to *ensure* that your business will fail. Don't start!

No business succeeds unless it begins. There are no statistics to which I can point, but I'm sure that far more businesses fail "because they never begin" than for any other reason.

You are ready to begin your business when you have a viable idea, a plan to finance the business, and a marketing strategy. You will have considered zoning and a price structure. Yet even when your are ready, your business cannot succeed if it remains in the planning stages. You have to get started. You may have all the reasons in the world for starting next month or next year. You may feel you need to do more research and still more research. Eventually, you must put all this behind you and take the plunge. You *must* get started.

The following is a list of books that will be helpful to you in starting, maintaining, and expanding your home business:

Cook, James R. *The Start-up Entrepreneur*. New York: Harper & Row, 1986.

Davidson, Jeffrey P. *Marketing for the Home-based Business*. Holbrook, Mass.: Bob Adams, 1990.

Eyler, David K. *Starting and Operating a Home-based Business*. New York: John Wiley & Sons, 1990.

Feldstein, Stuart. *Home, Inc.: How to Start and Operate a Successful Business from Your Home*. New York: Grosset & Dunlap, 1981.

Fleming, Lis. *The One-Minute Commuter*. Davis, Calif.: Acacia, 1989.

Gerber, Michael E. *The E Myth: Why Most Business Don't Work and What to Do About It*. Bullinger, 1986.

Holtz, Herman R. *Profit from Your Money-Making Ideas*. New York: Amacon, 1980.

Kern, Coralee Smith, and Tammara Hoffman Wolfgram. *Planning Your Own Home Business*. Lincolnwood, Ill.: VGM Career Horizons, 1989.

Lacey, Dan. *The Paycheck Disruption*. New York: Hippocrene, 1988.

Peterson, Judy. *Something of Your Own*. Wheaton, Ill.: Victor, 1991.

Simon, Julian L. *How to Start and Operate a Mail-Order Business*. 3d edition. New York: McGraw-Hill, 1981.

14
My Mommy and Daddy Work at Home

*H*ow successful are home businesses once they start? Business probably will be unsteady, even sluggish, during the first year or two. Of course, if you're married and your spouse is working, the limited earnings still add to the family income. If you're single, you should regard the slight income as something that can grow.

For instance, consider Randy Quinlain. After he lost his job as a teacher, he eventually began to offer investment counseling and to sell real estate. His first year was very slow.

"We went through a pretty tough time. My wife, Ronnie, found a job as a clerk at K-Mart, and I stayed home and took care of our boys. They were all preschool age back then. I applied for all sorts of jobs, but nothing turned up. About the only money I was making came from my job as a waiter on weekends.

"We really didn't want to look elsewhere for a job. Ronnie and I are both from this area, and we have most of our family here. We had our church friends as well. We wanted to stay.

"After looking for work the better part of a year, I decided to see whether I could do something on my own. I took some finance courses and a couple of courses in real estate. By this point, I had become accustomed to staying at home, and I realized that if I worked at it, I could establish myself as an independent investment counselor and sell real estate in the evenings and on weekends.

"It took a long time for me to build up these businesses. Income was really spotty, and I wasn't averaging more than a few hundred dollars a month. So, I studied to become credentialed as an insurance agent. Once I had my license, I started selling—mostly to people I had met as an investment counselor or real estate agent. This helped as well."

Today Randy runs a successful home business. As a matter of fact, he runs several. He's an investment counselor and an insurance agent. He sells real estate. And he writes appeal letters for several charitable organizations.

"I fell into the appeals-writing business almost by accident. I had a friend from church who worked for the local mission. Their secretary had been writing their appeal letters, and, quite frankly, she wasn't doing a very good job. When Jack, my friend, told me about this, I asked him if I could try my hand at it—strictly on a volunteer basis. After I volunteered, I wondered if I was crazy. After all, I had never written an appeal letter before. But I wrote it, and they liked it. Once I had written a couple, we agreed on a fee that I would be paid. My reputation spread by word of mouth. Within a year, I was writing the monthly letter for two other missions and for a couple other organizations as well.

"By now I was making enough that we could scrape by without Ronnie's job at K-Mart. She had worked there for over three years and really wanted to stay home with the kids. She suggested that maybe she could do something at home that would bring in some money. We both brainstormed for a while. She was a good seamstress and a great baker. We decided to try those angles. At first, she didn't make a whole lot. But gradually she built up her reputation, and soon she had more business than she could handle. We even got the boys helping her with her baking. And I do a lot of her deliveries when I come into town on business."

Randy and Ronnie reported income of more than $75,000 last year. They live comfortably with their three teen-age sons on the outskirts of a midsized Midwestern city.

"The Lord has certainly blessed us financially. But even if we were still just scraping by, I'd do it this way. We're busy, but we have a flexible schedule. When I'm not visiting a client or showing a house, I can dress the way I want. And the best part is that we can spend a lot of time together as a couple and as a family.

"I remember a few years back when Chad, our youngest, was asked at school to write down what his parents did for a living. Do you know what he wrote? 'My mommy and daddy work at home.' I kind of like that. He didn't know just what we did, but he knew we worked at home."

The Quinlains are part of a growing new wave—the home worker. Not all work at home out of necessity. Some are choosing it intentionally and voluntarily. But they all share one thing in common. They don't have to leave home to do their work.

They are part of the trend of the future. However, this trend has its roots in the past. Before the Industrial Revolution, most people worked at home. A high percentage of people worked on family farms. Many of those who lived in towns and cities owned shops—meat markets, fruit stands, cheese shops, dry goods stores, blacksmith shops, tanneries, and the like. Typically, these shops were storefronts. The family lived in back of the shop or upstairs. Whether on the farm or in the city, husband, wife, and children were all involved in the family business.

I f you are looking for a job, don't rule out looking at the home front. ... The stigma of staying home to work is lessening.

With the Industrial Revolution, all that changed. The change didn't come suddenly but gradually. Because of mechanized equipment, the size of the average farm increased from a few acres to hundreds of acres. As a result, fewer farmers were needed to till the soil. The blacksmith gave way to the foundry. The carriage maker was replaced by the automobile assembly plant. Shoes were no longer made by a cobbler working in his house but in a large factory. The dry goods store became the department store. The meat market, fruit stand, and tea and coffee store were consolidated into the supermarket. People stopped working at home and began commuting to a central workplace. By mid-twentieth century, this change was almost complete in the industrialized West.

Then the Information Revolution exploded. Computers led the way. More recently, facsimile transmissions, known as "faxes," and car phones have appeared. The file clerk and bookkeeper have become data entry operators. The secretary at the home office can fax her boss's report to the branch offices. A company can hire a person thousands of miles away to take its phone orders. People can communicate from halfway around the world as easily as if they were sitting at adjoining desks. The "electronic cottage" makes the centralized office superfluous for most tasks.

Many corporations have been slow to react to this revolution, mostly due to lethargy. But as certain more progressive companies lead the way, others will follow. Moreover, the self-employed worker, with powerful computers and communication tools easily within his financial grasp, will be able to offer many of the same services provided by larger firms. The centralized workplace will become the decentralized cottage once again.

If you are looking for a job, therefore, don't rule out looking at the home front. Many current employees are. The stigma of staying home is lessening, as both employer and employees see the advantages. The advantages are many. One is the *flexible schedule.* The home worker, whether self-employed or a telecommuter, can set his own schedule. Provided he gets his work done, he can awake when he wants to and go to bed when he wants. He can work four ten-hour days or even three thirteen-hour days each week. He can take a weekday morning off and work a half day on Saturday. He can work sixty hours two weeks in a row and then take an entire week off.

---

*T**he greatest advantage for the home worker is that the person has time to spend with his family.*

Moreover, he can work *more efficiently.* Anyone who has ever worked in an office knows how little work really gets done. Coffee breaks, conversations with fellow workers, and countless meetings (often conducted quite inefficiently) all waste time. The flow of work, once interrupted by these things, is very difficult to reestablish. The productivity of telecommuters is 15 to 30 percent higher than employees who work in an office. For the self-employed entrepreneur, that productivity is probably higher still.[9]

The home worker also *saves time and gas*. Both are precious commodities. A person who has even a twenty-minute one-way commute to work spends 160 hours commuting each year. That's four forty-hour work weeks. Someone with an hour's commute will spend 480 hours per year getting to and from work. This adds up to twelve forty-hour weeks. A home worker can use that extra time for work, for recreation, for his hobbies, for his church—for whatever he desires.

Gas is expensive. So is public transportation. A home worker doesn't have to worry about spending a minimum of $50 per month getting to and from work. He doesn't contribute to rush-hour traffic and wear and tear on the highways. Nor is he part of the problem of big-city air pollution.

The home worker *can dress the way he wants*—at least most of the time. Those who must see clients in their homes may have to dress up during their appointments. However, even then, slightly more casual clothing is acceptable in a home office than in a company office. Other home workers can dress pretty much however they want. They can wear tuxedos or evening gowns, blue jeans and T-shirts or nightgowns, and no one is going to care.

Unless he's a telecommuter, *the home worker isn't limited by a paycheck.* While he has no guarantee that he will make a particular salary, his potential for financial success is much greater than it would be otherwise.

However, the greatest advantage for the home worker is that the person has time to spend with his family. This is especially important for the Christian.

By being at home, a father and mother can go a long way toward ensuring the cohesiveness of the family.

Christians rightly decry the break-up of the family—the soaring divorce rate, the rebelliousness of children, the number of single-parent households. At the same time, these things are becoming increasingly common among believers. But what else should we expect? The Christian's household has become indistinguishable from the household of the unbeliever—both parents working outside the house, young children in day care or at the baby-sitter's, older children coming home from school to an empty house. Rarely does everyone in the family eat even one meal a day together, much less three. Dads may see their children for a few minutes a day—at most. Moms are sometimes just as scarce. Husband and wife are rarely together, except to sleep. If one of them works a late shift, they may not even be together then.

Working at home is not a panacea for all family problems. But by being at home, a father and mother can go a long way toward ensuring the cohesiveness of the family.

That is what Randy and Ronnie Quinlain have found. "By being at home I can help Ronnie with her work," says Randy. "She helps me as well. We've developed a sense of teamwork that we'd never have had otherwise."

"That's been my experience too," adds Ronnie. "If Randy were doing all his work outside the house, I wouldn't have any idea what he really did for a living, and I certainly wouldn't have any appreciation for his work. But, although I can't say I know the ins and outs of insurance or real estate, much less his investment counseling, I'm aware of a lot of what he's doing. And I can converse with him about his job in a meaningful way. At times I'm even able to advise him on certain important decisions."

Other couples report similar experiences. Five years ago, Mike McCarter lost his accounting job when his firm went bankrupt. He decided to begin a home-based accounting business. At about the same time, his wife Barb worked out a telecommuting arrangement with her employer, which allowed her to work at home four days a week.

"When we first decided to both work at home," says Barb, "we wondered whether we would get into each other's hair. We had a reasonably happy marriage, or so we thought, and we didn't want to do anything to create disharmony. Well, as it turned out, staying at home drew us closer. We have time to talk things out during the day. We share our goals and ideas, our worries and concerns. And, as we have seen each other work, our mutual respect has increased."

Being at home has a vital effect on the children as well. In Deuteronomy 6:6-9, we read that Moses told the children of Israel:

> These commandments that I give you today are to be upon your hearts. Impress them on your children. Talk about them when you sit at home and when you walk along the road, when you lie down and when you get up. Tie them as symbols on your hands and bind them on your foreheads. Write them on the doorframes of your houses and on your gates.

Just as the Israelites were to instruct their children in the law of Moses, we too are to faithfully teach our children the commands of the Bible. Proverbs 22:6 says, "Train a child in the way he should go, and when he is old he will not turn from it."

We cannot train our children in what the Bible says unless we spend time with them. And we certainly cannot give them that intimate and continual training that the Bible envisions unless we are with them frequently.

When parents are working at home, they have this opportunity. They can take time out to talk to their children. There is time for family Bible reading and prayer. Throughout the day, opportunities arise to show how Scripture applies to day-to-day life.

Children learn not only by precept but by example as well. As they see their parents hard at work, they learn the virtue of diligence. As they see them dealing honestly and fairly with customers, they learn these characteristics themselves. When they see their father or mother making sure a product doesn't leave the home unless it meets the highest standards, they learn the importance of a job well done.

In addition, when parents are at home, they are able to share their children's joy in the many small triumphs they experience each day. They can comfort their children when they're sad. They can attend to scraped knees and other small hurts. They can give a hug when needed. In a word, they can show the children that they're loved.

"Even if I knew I could make twice as much money working away from the home," says Randy Quinlain, "I wouldn't do it. I'd never trade what the Lord has given me the past twelve years. I've been with my boys day in and day out during that time. I know my children about as well as a human father can. I feel that being around them has been better than any material comfort I could ever give them. So why would I want to leave home now?"

Having had the privilege of spending many hours at home with my wife, and having watched our own children develop for nearly eight years, I couldn't agree more. I'm thankful I'm a stay-at-home dad. And I'm thankful that the ranks of home workers are swelling daily. I'm convinced that it will have a salutary effect on the family.

Not everyone can be a home worker, but if you are looking for another job, consider whether working at home might be a possibility. It may be just the tonic you need for your financial and physical health, your marriage, and, above all, your family.

PART **5**

SO YOU WANT TO HELP

15
Compassion Counts

*M*ick Johnson bundled his family into their van, took his position behind the steering wheel, and started the engine. The Johnson family was going to church, just as they did every other Sunday morning. There was only one difference. Mick was unemployed. The week before he had been a buyer for Western Printing and Supply Company. Now he felt like a nobody.

"I wasn't looking forward to going to church that Sunday," Mick admits. "Our congregation is pretty close-knit, and most of the regulars already knew. Peggy, my wife, had told her prayer group, and the rest had found out from them. I knew I'd get expressions of sympathy—almost as if someone had died. And people would offer advice like, 'Hang in there, Mick. I know you'll get another job soon.' I might even hear a story or two about someone's Uncle John who survived two years without a job. Small comfort that would be.

"And I was right. A few people at church either didn't know or didn't care. They acted as if nothing had happened. A couple others seemed to want to say something, but they couldn't or didn't. They just acted embarrassed. Then there were those who attempted to sympathize. One fellow actually acted as though he was at a funeral. I don't know which was worse, the sympathizers or those who tried to make me feel better by joking about it. All I know is that none of these people helped. I was angry, frustrated, and hurt, and I didn't need any of these reactions.

"Not everyone was like this. Don was really helpful. He told me that he was sorry to hear I had lost my job, mentioned that he was available to help, and gave me the names of a few friends he thought might be able to aid in my job search.

"Wanda, his wife, was also helpful. She knew that Peggy and I would both be looking for work, and she offered to baby-sit the kids if necessary. She also said that she'd talk to her boss to see if there were any openings.

"As it turned out, Wanda was able to get Peggy a part-time job in her office. Don's direct leads didn't result in a job for me. But one of the fellows he contacted knew someone else who eventually had an opening. Of course, that was a few months later. In the meantime, Don and Wanda continued to be supportive in every way.

"Some time later Peggy and I found out that Don had gone through a couple long periods of unemployment himself. That may explain his ability to understand."

Most people would like to help those who are going through an employment crisis. But like the people in Mick's church, they don't really know how. They can't fully understand the frustration, the anger, the apprehensiveness, the feeling of hopelessness a job crisis often brings. As a result, their attempts to help are woefully inadequate. These attempts may even do more harm than good.

Experience is often the best teacher. Someone who has gone through an employment crisis is probably better able to help others in a similar predicament. Perhaps you have never been unemployed or laid off. You may not have experienced more than the mildest form of job dissatisfaction. You may never have had to go through a career change. If so, you may wonder, "How can *I* help?"

Though you may not be able to experience all the emotions and turmoil that the person in a job crisis goes through, you can help. You can be sensitive to him. You can come to understand his needs. And you can help fill them.

As someone who has undergone two lengthy periods of unemployment, I'd like to offer several suggestions. If you follow these, you should be better able to aid those who are going through a job crisis.

DON'T CONDEMN

Mark Benjamin was a rising executive in a large corporation in the transportation industry when he began to suffer job burnout. For the sake of his health, his sanity, and his family, he quit his job and took a part-time position as a clerk in a local department store. To help support the family, his wife, Mary, found employment as a receptionist in a dentist's office. Because they lived in a fairly modest home, they continued to make their mortgage payments and had enough left over to meet their other obligations.

"I can't say that we had it easy," says Mark, "but with our combined income we continued to make ends meet. The problem wasn't so much with us, but with the reaction of our friends. I absolutely had to get away from what I was doing. I had been working sixty to seventy hours a week. My health was suffering, and I hardly knew my family. I needed time off. But it seemed that no one really understood this.

"Oh, I suppose that there were some sympathetic people. But lots of people simply scratched their heads. And I'm not just talking about the men with whom I worked. I'm talking about family members and people in the church as well. They couldn't fathom how I could leave such a great job.

"I guess I can understand this. If you've never been on the corporate fast track, you see only the benefits—the salary, the prestige, the title, the potential. You don't see the long hours, the exhaustion, the evenings and weekends away from the family. So maybe you can't figure out why I'd throw this all away."

While Mick Johnson suffered through condolences and a sense of gloom at church, Mark found people critical. They did not always voice their criticism. But in their confusion as to how an able-bodied man—and father—could leave a full-time job, their negative attitude was obvious.

Condemnation can be very subtle. Even so, if you have a condemning attitude toward another person, that attitude will show through. You don't have to say "You lazy, no-good oaf. Why don't you get a job?" for someone to know that you feel that way.

Mark found the critical attitude tough to handle. "It wasn't just that they thought I was crazy to leave the job, but that I was *wrong*. I had people tell me that I shouldn't have let my wife go out to work, that I was jeopardizing my family's welfare, and that I was shirking my responsibilities. One fellow even told me that I was just plain lazy. And all this at a time when I felt a little compassion wouldn't hurt."

SHOW COMPASSION

Compassion counts. The person who is going through an employment crisis already has a fragile psyche. The last thing he needs is condemnation. Even if you don't understand his or her decision, show compassion. Give the benefit of the doubt.

Most people lose their jobs through no fault of their own. They aren't defective just because they're unemployed. Furthermore, they aren't crazy just because they do not take the first job that comes along.

Maybe they aren't even looking very hard for another job. This doesn't mean they're lazy. The shock of losing a job can be debilitating. An unemployed person may be going through an intense struggle without anyone else knowing it. Plus, he or she may have deep feelings of failure or rejection. It isn't surprising that the unemployed are sometimes so defeated that they don't even appear to be interested in finding another job.

Your attitude, then, should be one of charity, not condemnation. Otherwise, you won't get to first base with a person going through a job crisis.

BE AVAILABLE TO HELP

"When I lost my job," says Merle Friesen, "I found out there were three types of people. There were those who didn't care, those who said they cared but did nothing, and those who *really* cared. Plenty of people told me how tough I had it or how bad I must be feeling. They were right. But I didn't need them to tell me this. I knew it already.

"And there were those who said, 'If there's anything I can do, let me know.' But I could tell they didn't really mean it. I asked two of these people for help, and guess what? They turned me down.

"And then I had my *real* friends. Some of them told me they wanted to help. Others didn't have to say anything. I simply knew I could depend on them. In either case, when I did ask for something, they did whatever they could. These were the people who helped me through my time of unemployment."

You can help in many different ways. Sometimes the person going through a job crisis needs someone to talk to. You don't have to be an expert in career counseling to listen. You may even feel incompetent to give advice. Leave that to others. Just be available to listen.

Hints for Helps

Someone in your church or neighborhood has lost or left a job. He faces frustration, fear, and worry while seeking new employment. Your words and works can help him through the interim. Here are several ways you can help.

1. *Be a good listener.* A good ear allows your friend to articulate his fears and know that someone cares. He may even be able to sort through some options verbally as you listen quietly. You don't have to be an expert in career counseling to listen.
2. *Host the family.* Invite the unemployed and his or her family to dinner. Your home can provide an atmosphere for play and conversation, as well as a welcome meal outside their home. That dinner also can build the relationship for later personal contacts.
3. *Offer clothes.* Your used clothing—in good condition—may help your neighbors stretch their budget. Your children can donate clothing they have outgrown. They also can learn about true giving when they donate lesser worn outfits from their current wardrobe.
4. *Give groceries.* Consider food gifts from time to time. A generous supply of food basics, such as canned vegetables, soups, pasta, sauces, and eggs, can help greatly.
5. *Be a volunteer.* Offer your skills in home or auto repair to save the person money and valuable time. If the unemployed has children, you can volunteer one day for child care, letting the person prepare résumés or do research at the library.

If your friend has young children at home and needs to go to job interviews, you can offer to baby-sit. You may even want to volunteer your baby-sitting services to give your friend time to send out résumés or make phone calls. Your help may prove invaluable.

A job crisis—particularly unemployment—can bring financial hardships. This can be a touchy subject. The person you're trying to help may be too proud to admit that he or she is having financial difficulties. That person may be too proud to accept charity. You have to be sensitive. However, if your friend is willing to accept help, there's a lot you can do.

If you have second-hand clothes in good condition, you can offer these. This form of assistance may be particularly welcomed by someone with fast-growing children. You may want to consider food gifts from time to time. Monetary assistance is another matter. Many people who are happy to receive food and clothing are embarrassed at the thought of taking money. It reeks too much of direct charity. So be very careful about monetary gifts. Don't give them unless you know that the person is willing to accept them. However, anonymous gifts usually cause no problems.

If you're mechanically minded, you can volunteer your services to help repair things that have broken down—a car, for instance. An unemployed person needs his car, particularly for job interviews, so if you're adept at automotive repairs, you might want to repair it for him, thus saving him an expensive repair bill.

These are just a few of the ways you can help. There are many more. The most important piece of advice I can give is this: Be sensitive to the person's needs. If you are, you'll see many things you can do.

BE PART OF THE NETWORKING PROCESS

When Bill Lemke lost his job after fifteen productive years, he didn't know what to do. "I was a complete novice," says Bill. "I had no idea how to construct a résumé. I didn't know what a cover letter was. I was overwhelmed by the want ads. And I really had very few contacts, or so I thought.

"If it weren't for my friends at church, I don't know what I would have done. They pulled me through. One of them was really good at writing résumés. As a result, I was able to list a whole slew of qualifications I'd have otherwise overlooked. Another one volunteered to type some of my cover letters, and even suggested how I might word them.

"But the biggest help came from all the people who gave me job leads. If you confine your search to the want ads, you're cutting out most of the job opportunities. But I had several friends who kept their eyes and ears open. Before long, I had several promising leads and some interviews lined up. Some of these wound up being dead ends. But that doesn't really matter. It only takes one yes to get a job. And that yes came as a result of a lead I received from a friend in my church."

You may not be good at counseling people. You may not even be a particularly good listener. And you may be too pressed for time or money yourself to help someone in other ways. But you can almost always help in the networking process. It's not hard to be aware of the openings and potential openings where you work. In fact, it's hard not to be aware of them. And, with a little effort, you can usually find out about openings in other companies. For instance, you can quiz salesmen or people with whom you deal on the phone.

Your friend Jill, a secretary now without a job, needs contacts. She knows you and you know people in other companies who have or soon will have openings due to transfers or retirements. You tell Jill. This is networking.

Your coworkers may also be a source of leads. If you don't turn up something immediately, keep at it. Sooner or later you will become aware of some job openings out there. When you do, pass them on to Jill.

If you've recently been through a job search yourself, you're in a position to offer some practical advice. Networking includes giving the unemployed helpful advice based on your experience and personal contacts. Like Bill Lemke's friend, you might have become a good résumé writer. If so, sit down with the person going through a job crisis and help him with his résumé. If you've become adept at being interviewed, explain what you've learned. Your advice might prove immeasurably helpful. If you know how to differentiate promising leads from those likely to result in dead ends, express this insight as well. Remember, information is useless only if it isn't shared.

DON'T WAIT FOR THE UNEMPLOYED TO REQUEST YOUR HELP

When I left the pastorate and my family and I moved back to Lincoln, we immediately started attending the church that would become our church home. Most of the members became aware of our situation almost immediately. Very few, however, did much to help. And most showed little concern. I often wondered why that was.

After being back for nearly two years I got a clue. A woman in our congregation happened to read an article that I wrote about my response to being unemployed. Afterward she told Elizabeth that she had "no idea how hard it had been for us."

As I thought about it, I realized that I had given her no reason to believe that we were going through any sort of struggle. In fact, I had given no one in our church any reason to believe this. I tend to be an extremely self-contained person. I don't wear my feelings on my sleeve. I seldom share my needs with others. And I hate to ask anyone for help—ever.

This is true of most people in a job crisis. Many believe that asking for help is a sign of weakness. "I've gotten into it myself, and I want to get out of it myself," is a typical, if unconscious, attitude. This message is conveyed to others, who simply assume that he or she is getting along "OK."

But things *aren't* OK. The person in a job crisis needs help—your help. You need to be sensitive to this. He or she probably won't ask for your help—or anyone else's help, for that matter. But don't be fooled. Though everything may appear to be fine, that doesn't mean it is.

Even when someone does not indicate his specific need, you can help the person in a job crisis in a couple ways. For instance, mention a job opening you've heard about or an upcoming career-assessment seminar. Let him or her know you are willing to listen, and then do so. If the person is married, try talking to the spouse. A person in an employment crisis might be unwilling to call out for help. But that person's husband or wife might not share this reluctance.

In any case, don't go by outward appearances. A job crisis is just that—a crisis. A person in crisis needs help. Approach him with that attitude. You may have to take the first step.

BE AWARE OF THE TENSION

Barry Lohmeier's eyes sparkle. His spontaneous laughter fills a room. That's why his description of himself when he was unemployed seems incongruous.

"I was a real grouch," he says, chuckling a bit at a memory that has surely been softened with time. "And I was especially nasty when people tried to help. I don't know just why, but they grated on me the wrong way.

"I remember when my next door neighbor told me about an opening down at the plant where he worked. I think I practically roared at him, 'Why don't you go work in an employment agency!' That was the last time he tried to help. I can't blame him.

"Then there was a couple at church who got wind that we were going through a really hard time. They had us over to dinner and afterwards gave my wife a couple bags of clothes for the children to wear. Sandy thanked them several times. Me? I just stormed off and got into the car. Sandy took the brunt of my anger on that occasion. I really lit into her about accepting charity from anyone.

"Eventually I learned to accept help. But before that, I'm sure I hurt a lot of feelings. I just hope that everyone realizes it wasn't anything personal."

The person in a job crisis is going through a tough time emotionally. Anger and frustration run high. This means that when you offer to help, you may be rebuffed. In his frustration, he becomes irritable and tense. You must realize that "it isn't anything personal."

It's never easy being rebuffed. When we are, our initial reaction is to say, "I'll never help that person again." This reaction is understandable. But it doesn't absolve us from our ongoing duty.

Our motivation in helping a person in a job crisis should not be to receive praise or thanks. If it is, more often than not, we're going to be sorely disappointed. Some people will be grateful. When they are, we can praise God. Others, however, will forget to thank us. We may even encounter their anger and hostility. When we do, we'll be tempted to give up on them. But if our motivation is not to receive thanks but to truly be a servant, we will press on. We will realize that the rebuff we receive, the anger and frustration we encounter, is good evidence that the person really does need our help.

Moreover, although their anger may boil over, those who are going through a job crisis are not going to be angry all the time. They are more likely to be like Barry Lohmeier. After a time, they will realize that you really are trying to help. And they will accept your help. So, even if you are rebuffed, persevere. Your willingness to help will eventually be appreciated.

REMEMBER THE EMOTIONS

It's easy to understand the financial ramifications of a job crisis. And it's relatively simple to tell a person how to go about getting another job. A financial adviser can deal with the former, and a job counselor can do the latter. Far too often, however, the emotional implications of a job crisis are forgotten. Nevertheless, before a person can handle the practical aspects of a job crisis, that person needs to come to grips with his or her emotions.

Remember, the unemployed face many emotions. The loss of a job can bring *grief.* This grief may not be as intense or overwhelming as the grief felt when a loved one dies. But it *is* grief—real grief—nonetheless.

Job dissatisfaction as well as job loss can bring *confusion.* An individual may be utterly uncertain what to do next. The more options available the more bewildered he may be.

A job crisis may result in loss of self-esteem, even in a *feeling of total incompetence.* Or it may result in *anger*—anger at an employer, anger at family, anger at God.

A whole range of emotions and attitudes are likely to be seething right under the surface. If you are to help a person during a job crisis, you need to be aware of these. And you need to help that person deal with these feelings.

You will be able to do this only if you are extremely sensitive. Listen carefully to what he or she is saying. Sally, for instance, may not say that she's angry, but she might talk about how unfairly she's been dealt with. Dick may not admit to suffering loss of self-esteem. At the same time, he may state that he doesn't think that he's really qualified for anything.

Becky may not shed a tear, but she may speak longingly of a job she has lost. It's up to you to *listen* and to *discern*.

If you succeed in this, you will be able to help such people deal with their feelings and emotions. That may be the greatest service you can render to someone going through a job crisis.

16
What the Church Can Do

*A*dam Brenley's bear-like frame more than filled the chair in Pastor Kingsley's study. His booming voice and hearty laugh echoed off the wall. As he talked, he rocked back and forth. As he usually did when Adam paid a visit, Steve Kingsley began to speculate on how much a new office chair would cost. *I wonder if the present one would make good firewood*, he joked to himself. But Steve soon put light thoughts aside. What Adam was talking about was far too intriguing—and somber.

Adam had been describing his travails during the five-month period he had been laid off from his construction job. As usual, he could see the lighter side of even the worst of circumstances. But suddenly, he shifted gears. His voice became higher-pitched and staccato. Steve knew this meant that Adam was serious and extremely excited about something.

"Reverend," boomed Adam, "we gotta do something about all the other guys in the church who don't have jobs. Praise God I got one now. But when I was laid off, I told God I was gonna do something to help them guys. You got Jim and Tony Moreno. They've been outta work for nearly a year now. And I don't think the soup plant's gonna hire 'em back. And Tim Yarsa's outta work at the steel mill. Kelly's Lumber Yard laid off Tom Beauchamp a few weeks back. And Angie Hriniak didn't get her teaching contract renewed, so she doesn't have a job this fall. She doesn't know how she's going to support her kids."

Adam continued, listing the names on his fingers. For a fleeting second, Steve thought Adam might start on his toes next. But Adam simply started over on his fingers. After a couple of minutes, Adam's list had grown to more than twenty names. Although Steve was the senior pastor at Oak Lake Community Church, he had never realized how many people in the congregation were unemployed. A couple of the men Adam listed had never even told Steve, and he was quite unaware that they didn't have jobs.

His list completed, Adam paused for breath. Steve could tell that Adam was really about to get on a roll. When Adam got going, there was no point interrupting him.

Your church can be an Oak Lake Church. It requires only compassion, a vision, and a little organization.

"Reverend," Adam started again. His voice was more staccato than before, and the high pitch belied the heavy man's seriousness. "Reverend, we *gotta* do something. And I got an idea. I was thinking when I didn't have a job how great it would be to get together with other guys like me and let it all hang out. I'd of liked a chance to tell someone how angry I was, how scared, how I thought I might never work again. I'd of liked a chance to know there were other guys in the same boat as me. And I think these other guys wanna have a chance to do the same. We gotta start what I think they call a support group."

Adam kept going. The more he talked, the more Steve realized that Oak Lake needed to get involved. It needed a ministry to the men and women of the church who were unemployed.

By lunchtime, Adam and Steve had drawn up a plan. They would begin a support group. It would meet for the first time the next Tuesday morning and would be open not only to the unemployed but to anyone who was interested in helping in any way. Adam volunteered to bring plenty of doughnuts and sweet rolls, and Steve promised to make sure that the church secretary brewed a couple pots of coffee.

The story of the support group of Oak Lake Community Church could be that of any church. In fact such groups exist in many churches. The descriptions in this chapter are a compilation of and expansion upon methods various congregations are using to deal with unemployment and other job crises. It represents a vision of what a church can do rather than what any particular church is doing.

Your church can be an Oak Lake Church. It requires only compassion, a vision, and a little organization, as you will see in this story of Oak Lake.

The Sunday bulletin announcement and some phone calls by Adam and Pastor Steve had brought out about thirty men and women this cold but clear Tuesday morning. Most were members of Oak Lake. The rest had heard about the meeting from someone who attended the church. Of the thirty in attendance that morning, twenty-two were unemployed. The rest, including Adam and Pastor Steve, were there for support.

After a time chatting over coffee and doughnuts, the pastor suggested that everyone gather around in a circle. He then introduced himself to the nonmembers and turned the meeting over to Adam. At first slowly and with some stuttering, but then with increasing speed and easiness, Adam began to tell his story. He talked about the crushing blow his self-esteem had suffered as a result of being out of work, the financial hardship his family had suffered, the difficulty of a high-school dropout being out of a job, and the anger and frustration he had felt.

At times, when he touched on an area where his wounds were still fresh, tears flowed down his cheeks. Adam talked for more than half an hour. His speech wasn't eloquent, but it was spellbinding.

When he finished, there was a brief pause. Then Tony Moreno began to speak. At first he hesitated while speaking, and seemed calm. However, his anger began to show through as he started describing the strain being out of work had placed on his marriage and his family life. By the time he finished, he was trembling with rage—rage at his situation, at the government, and even at God.

Next it was Mary Sweeney's turn. Mary, a single mom, had lost her job when the local auto plant had cut back its work force six months earlier. Other than some part-time waitressing, she hadn't worked since. Crying almost the whole time, she told of how she often went without meals so her children could eat, how their clothes were falling apart, and how she had to find a much smaller, cramped apartment in the poorest section of town.

For nearly three hours that Tuesday morning, the men and women present released their pent-up emotions. A few had to leave before the meeting was over, but most stayed till the end. Those who did admitted that they were surprised at how intensely they had expressed their feelings. But they also agreed that the meeting had been therapeutic. They all wanted to meet again.

That evening, Adam called Steve at home. "Pastor," he began, "that was some great meeting. And that's just the start. I got some more ideas.

"We gotta find a way to get you and the church elders more involved with the lives of these people. And we gotta figure out how to help their families. And we need some way of helping them over the hump financially. And some of these folks need to learn how to go about getting another job. And they need to know where jobs are available. And—"

Steve's head began to swim. The very thought of the church running a full-blown employment service overwhelmed him. But he had to admit that what Adam was saying made sense. Based on that morning's meeting, unemployment was one of the most pressing problems facing the people at Oak Lake. In this area, the church certainly could make an impact in the lives of its people as well as in the community.

Pastor Steve agreed to give Adam's ideas further thought and to help where possible. He also thanked Adam for all the work he had already done and urged him to continue the program.

As the weeks and the months wore on, the two men, with the support and input of the church board, began Oak Lake's ministry to the unemployed. At first, they concentrated on strengthening the support groups. Within three months, four separate groups, each consisting of between twelve and fifteen members, were meeting at the church twice a month.

Next came a program of diaconal assistance. Adam and Steve decided that the ideal person to head up this ministry was Gregg Carver. Gregg was possibly the best deacon at Oak Lake. A real go-getter, Gregg was always bubbling with creative ideas. What's more, he had gone through a lengthy period of unemployment a couple years earlier. Under Gregg's enthusiastic guidance, the diaconal program expanded to include not only financial assistance, but a food pantry, a job-referral service, and even a "workfare" arrangement for the unemployed in the church and community.

Almost six months after Adam had first met with Steve, the final phase of the Oak Lake program began. One of the associate pastors, Kevin Savage, had worked in an employment agency before entering the ministry. He was the perfect choice to head up the Oak Lake employment counseling service. When he was first approached by Steve, he was a bit reluctant. He knew that to do the job right, he would have to put in a tremendous amount of effort. Already he was overworked in his role as pastor of adult ministries and Christian education; yet he could see the excitement that the ministry to the unemployed had already generated. After lengthy deliberation, Kevin agreed to take on this added responsibility.

Over a period of several weeks, Kevin read everything he could concerning résumé writing, career counseling, talent assessment, and the like. He then constructed detailed outlines of the material to be covered in various job-counseling seminars. In addition, he created the instructional material for these seminars. Finally, he crafted brochures to be used in advertising the seminars and the service to the church and the community.

The first seminar—how to hunt for a job—was a moderate success. The second—how to sell yourself to a potential employer—attracted even more people from the church and community. And the third was a winner in every sense. Entitled "How to Find Contentment in the Workplace," the seminar dealt with the underlying needs of every worker and drew a large gathering. The Oak Lake ministry to the unemployed was now in full swing.

That was two years ago. Today Oak Lake's ministry is still going strong. It has been responsible for helping more than fifty Oak Lake members through their job crises. In addition, it has brought many previously unchurched people into contact with Oak Lake. More than twenty-five people have become members as a direct result of this ministry, and others attend Oak Lake regularly.[10] Steve Kingsley still has oversight of the entire ministry. Gregg Carver still heads the diaconal program. Kevin Savage continues to expand the employment counseling service. And, of course, Adam Brenley is still involved. He leads a support group and provides ongoing inspiration for everyone.

The Oak Lake Community Church program provides a model for what the church can do to help its members and the community during times of job crises. Let's highlight and expand on the major aspects of its program.

SUPPORT GROUPS

The easiest way any church can help people through their job crises is by starting one or more support groups. Oak Lake Community Church in effect began its first group with that Tuesday morning meeting. It may be tempting to assume that all that needs to be done is to place a bulletin announcement, contact a few people, and have some coffee and doughnuts on hand. That may be a start, but much more needs to be done.

A support group needs a leader. Otherwise, the group is merely a bunch of people who happen to be in the same room and have a similar problem. In the Oak Lake program, two requirements were almost immediately set down for being a leader. First, the leader needed to be a committed member of the church, well acquainted with its teachings and practices. Second, he needed either to have been unemployed himself or to have been closely touched by unemployment (for example, through the unemployment of another member of the family).

The leader needs to understand the special problems encountered by people who are going through a job crisis. As the Oak Lake program evolved, potential leaders received a period of training from seasoned veterans. This training consisted of four one-hour sessions. Without this sort of training, the leader could find himself ill-equipped to deal with the emotions expressed by the members of the group.

As much as possible, spouses and other family members should become involved. At first, Oak Lake didn't fully see the need for this. As time went on, however, Adam, Steve, and the other leaders began to understand the extent to which an employment crisis is a *family* problem. Once they realized this, they encouraged family members to attend.

T   *he goal of support groups should be to get the individual to deal with his emotions, to accept his situation, and to learn to rely on the Lord for strength.*

Church members who are not directly involved in an employment crisis should become part of these groups. Remember, they are support groups: church members should be present to undergird those who are in need. The Oak Lake program required that each of its elders become involved in one support group. These men were able to lend maturity, encouragement, and insight to those in the group.

Each support group should be kept small. The thirty who attended the first Oak Lake meeting made for a situation that was unwieldy. Once the group quickly divided into sub-groups, the interactions increased among those present. An ideal number for a support group is probably between ten to fifteen. If there are more, people begin to feel that their needs as individuals aren't being met. Moreover, some people tend to become inhibited in large groups.

The purpose of the support groups should not be simply to provide a forum for people to vent their anger and frustration. Doing this may be therapeutic, but it shouldn't be the final product. The goal should be to get the individual to deal with his emotions, to accept his situation, and to learn to rely on the Lord for strength. The leader of the group must work to facilitate this in the case of each individual. That is one reason he needs to be trained for his role.

Finally, the support groups should reach into the community. If unemployment is a problem within a congregation, it is likely to be a problem in the community. Oak Lake is located in an economically depressed part of the country. Its own congregation reflects a critical problem in the city and even the state in which it is located. An affluent congregation in a well-to-do community may not have this problem. Many of its people, however, may be suffering from job burnout. Whatever the problem is, the church needs to provide an outreach that will minister to the needs of the surrounding community.

DIACONAL ASSISTANCE

When Steve Kingsley put Deacon Gregg Carver in charge of the deacons' assistance for the unemployed, he never dreamed that Gregg would implement such a diverse program. Gregg began simply enough. He persuaded the board of deacons to set aside funds for the unemployed who were enduring a severe financial crisis. In addition, he started a special food pantry designed specifically to help the families of unemployed individuals.

But Gregg didn't stop there. As a student of human nature, he was firmly convinced that flat-out charity has a debilitating effect on individuals. Moreover, he interpreted the Old Testament laws, particularly those relating to gleaning and indentured servanthood, as indicating that people should work in exchange for welfare. He felt his belief was further supported by the rule Paul gave to the Thessalonian Christians: "If a man will not work, he shall not eat" (2 Thessalonians 3:10).

Accordingly, Gregg went to the church board and asked its members to give him a list of all the repair and clean-up projects that needed to be done around the church. In addition, he sought out the church secretary, the Sunday school superintendent, the custodian, and just about anyone else who would listen, and asked them to make a list of jobs that needed to be done. Armed with this list, he began his own program of "workfare."

Gregg decided to press none of this upon the unemployed of the church or the community. He figured that some unemployed people would have other sources of income; others would simply not want to take advantage of this service, perhaps preferring to live on their unemployment benefits until they ran out. But Gregg aggressively advertised the church's service. Not only did he run an announcement in the Sunday bulletin, but he advertised on bulletin boards in the church and the community that Oak Lake had jobs available for unemployed people.

Because this was a new idea, the initial response was slow. But soon, the trickle of people who came looking for work became a steady stream. Gregg gave all applicants a choice. They could work for a flat hourly fee, or they could exchange their services for food from the church's pantry. The majority chose to work for money, but a significant number "bought" food with their work as well.

Because he wanted to treat these workers fairly, Gregg set payment well above the minimum wage. Depending on the skill involved, Gregg had the church pay anywhere from five to seven dollars an hour. To make sure there was enough work to go around, Gregg limited any one person to twenty hours of work per week. As the number of applicants increased, he had to reduce the limit to fifteen hours. Still, a worker could earn one hundred dollars a week this way. Gregg knew that this was hardly enough to support a family, but it might be just what someone would need to get over the hump. More importantly, those who were in the program were able to keep their dignity, for they were not simply accepting a handout.

Before long, many long-neglected repairs had been taken care of. The church grounds looked better than they had in years. The office files were in perfect order, and so was the church library. Gregg began to fear that the church would run out of jobs. But, somehow or other, new jobs kept coming in. It seemed there was always something to be done.

At about this time, the church secretary hinted that she could use some help. Gregg checked with the church board to see if there was enough money for a part-time position. There was. Gregg put up an advertisement for a woman with secretarial skills. The only other requirement for the position was that she or her husband be unemployed. Within a day, the church secretary had her helper.

For some time, Oak Lake had thought about starting a licensed day-care service. Gregg hadn't been especially enthusiastic about this project. But now he saw it as a perfect opportunity to help the unemployed. He knew that the day-care director would have to be a licensed operator. However, she would need helpers. Gregg knew that these could be unemployed single women or wives of unemployed men. Largely as a result of Gregg's enthusiastic effort, Oak Lake opened its day-care within three months. A full-time director and four part-time helpers were hired. Two of these helpers were single moms who were out of work. The other two were wives of unemployed men.

Once Gregg had Oak Lake's workfare program running smoothly, he turned his attention to what he believed was the other essential aspect of the diaconal program—a job-referral service. Gregg knew that workfare was simply a stopgap measure for the unemployed. Eventually, they needed to get a full-time, steady job.

Gregg was aware that Kevin Savage was working on Oak Lake's employment counseling service. He didn't want to duplicate his efforts. However, he knew that not only did people need to learn *how* to apply for jobs but also *where* the jobs were. Gregg decided to make this task as easy as possible for the unemployed in the church and the community.

*T*he Oak Lake job referral service . . . included seeking job listings from members . . . and posting three-by five cards with job openings on a church bulletin board.

Gregg's time was already at a premium. Besides all he was doing at the church, he was also holding down a full-time job. Still, he felt a job-referral service was absolutely crucial if Oak Lake was to provide the sort of help the unemployed needed. Somehow, he managed to squeeze out an hour here, a couple there. Before long, the Oak Lake job-referral service began to take shape.

Once again, Gregg placed an announcement in the church bulletin. This time he asked congregational members to let him know of any job openings they were aware of. To ensure that the information was as accurate and as complete as possible, Gregg typed up and ran off an information form. This form contained a space for the job title, description, company, address, telephone number, contact person, starting date, and salary. Whenever Gregg received a form from anyone in the church, he called the company to verify the existence of the job and the accuracy of the information.

In addition, Gregg contacted the personnel departments of the major employers in town. He familiarized them with Oak Lake's program and asked them to make their list of job openings available. A number of them cooperated. Gregg even scoured the want ads every day. When he found a job that appeared halfway promising, he added it to his list.

Gregg's next step was to get the church board to purchase a huge bulletin board; here he posted three-by five cards with job openings, arranged by category. He also color-coded these cards according to the area of the city in which the jobs were located. He placed the board prominently near the front entrance to the church.

Besides this, Gregg's wife constructed a booklet that listed these jobs. As an unemployed person came to the church for assistance, he was given a copy of the booklet to aid him in his job search. Gregg decided to update this booklet biweekly to keep its job listings as current as possible.

Gregg asked for just one thing of the unemployed in return for the use of this service. As soon as they were hired, they were to notify him. This allowed him to strike these jobs from the list when they were filled. Occasionally, a person forgot, but most were happy to do this as a token of their gratitude.

EMPLOYMENT COUNSELING

Starting a support group or a program of diaconal assistance is fairly straightforward. Employment counseling is another matter. A church should not attempt to do this unless a person with some experience in the area is available. Oak Lake Community Church had such a person in Kevin Savage. Even he felt the need for further study before offering his advice to the unemployed. A rank amateur can do far more harm than good.

That does not mean that a church without an expert on its staff or in the congregation should rule out the possibility of employment counseling entirely. It has two options. One or more members of the church can get training in this area, or it can bring in Christian employment and career counselors to conduct seminars and workshops. Both options will cost the church money. Outside professionals do not come free. If the church is going to commission its members to get training, it should pay for their tuition, their time, and eventually their services. This said, let's note some employment counseling services the church can offer.

Résumé Writing

Kevin Savage knew from his experience in an employment agency that very few people had any idea how to construct a résumé. One of his first tasks was to set up a résumé-writing service. Most of the people who came to the church for help couldn't afford the fee the professional services in town were charging. Kevin offered the same service for free. When his workload began to increase, he trained a couple of women from the church to be his assistants. They did most of the résumés, but left the difficult ones for him.

Interview Preparation

Most job applicants don't know how to handle a job interview. The interview, however, is often much more crucial than the applicant's qualifications in determining whether he or she gets the job. A prospective employer can tell only so much from reading a résumé and contacting references. His decision on whether he can work with a prospective employee is almost entirely determined by the impression left by the interview.

That is why one of the first seminars that Kevin gave at Oak Lake was on how to sell yourself to a prospective employer. In this seminar, he focused heavily on the interview process itself. As time went on, he repeated this seminar and eventually began giving it on a monthly basis. In addition, he offered to "prep" individuals for a specific interview if they felt this would help them in their performance.

Talent Assessment

Oak Lake Community Church had an advantage. Kevin Savage was already familiar with various talent-assessment tests and programs. He was able to use these in his seminars and his one-on-one counseling with individuals who came to the church for help.

However, it is possible for the church to offer this service without a Kevin Savage in its midst. Many books on career counseling contain tests and exercises ideally suited for use in a small-group setting. As part of its employment counseling ministry, a church may want to set up various small groups to study one or more of these books. Ideally, the leaders of these groups should have some training in this area. At the very least, they should have done the exercises in several of these books themselves. (See chapter 5 for a brief list of relevant books.)

CAREER COUNSELING

Unemployment is only one form of employment crisis. As noted earlier in this book, many people are utterly unhappy in their jobs. They too are going through a job crisis and stand in need of career counseling. Unfortunately, good career counseling requires a person with considerable training in the field. A career counselor needs to be familiar with talent-assessment exercises and know how to interpret them. He also must be able to match talents and personality types with various careers. If he can't do this, or does a bad job of it, he'll hurt rather than help the people who use his services.

However, as indicated earlier, the church can bring in Christian professional career counselors to conduct seminars and workshops. It can also do something similar to what Kevin Savage did at Oak Lake. Kevin knew that with all his other duties he wouldn't have time to give individual career counseling to everyone who came to Oak Lake for help. He decided to buy several "self-help" books on the subject and place them in Oak Lake's career counseling center. In addition, he purchased a number of books on specific careers. People who desired career counseling could check out these books. Those who took advantage of this service were often able to make informed decisions concerning their career without seeking further counseling (see the chapter 5 bibliography for helpful books).

Not every congregation has the resources .. to do all that Oak Lake has done. But every congregation is called to be sensitive to those ... who are caught in the job shuffle.

The ministry of Oak Lake Community Church serves as a model of what the church can do for those who are in a job crisis. Not every congregation is called to this sort of ministry. And, certainly, not every congregation has the resources or the personnel to do all that Oak Lake has done. But every congregation is called to be sensitive to those in its midst who are caught in the job shuffle.

Like a city on a hill, the church of Jesus Christ is to be a beacon of light to the world around it. Its light shines forth not only as it proclaims the gospel but as it ministers to the temporal needs of those who look to it for help. The upheaval of the work force will accelerate in the years ahead as the West continues to move from the Industrial to the Informational Age. One of the greatest ministries the church can have will be to those who will be occupationally displaced.

Afterword 1

"But the Bible Says . . ."

hristmas Eve 1989. We had been back in Lincoln nearly ten months, long enough to join a church, make friends, and be settled in our new life. Others had had time to size up our situation. We were conversing with a young man from our church who was spending the day with us.

"I've heard lots of favorable comments about your preaching and teaching, Doug," Jim began. "Your gifts are generally recognized. But there's some question about your qualifications as an elder—"

Jim paused momentarily. And then, "A number of people wonder about your staying at home while Elizabeth is working."

Jim quickly added that he didn't share this doubt. But, once again, the issue had arisen. Was I doing something wrong by letting Elizabeth work while I took care of the children? Was our lifestyle unbiblical?

Just what does the Bible say about this? Before Elizabeth went out to work, we never thought too much about the issue. We simply assumed that the Bible tells men to go out to work and tells women to stay home and rear the children. Finding ourselves in this topsy-turvy situation, we had to re-open God's Word.

My wife and I decided to look first at the "male headship" passages and then at those that speak of the office of elder. If none of these supported our presuppositions, we were determined to find anything else—Old Testament or New—even remotely related to the issue.

In 1 Corinthians 11:3 we read, "Now I want you to realize that the head of every man is Christ, and the head of the woman is man, and the head of Christ is God." Paul makes these remarks as part of a discussion of propriety in worship. Not surprisingly, then, he doesn't go on to relate this comment in any way to the question of who should be the family's breadwinner.

The other frequently cited male-headship passage is Ephesians 5:22-24: "Wives, submit to your husbands as to the Lord. For the husband is the head of the wife as Christ is the head of the church, his body, of which he is the Savior. Now as the church submits to Christ, so also wives should submit to their husbands in everything."

A few verses later Paul adds, "In this same way, husbands ought to love their wives as their own bodies. He who loves his wife loves himself. After all, no one ever hated his own body, but he feeds and cares for it, just as Christ does the church" (vv. 28-29). This is the only statement in the entire passage (vv. 22-33) that could possibly be construed as having anything to do with being the family breadwinner.

Paul, however, is *not* saying "Husbands, just as you love your own bodies by feeding and caring for them, so you should love your wives by providing food for them (that is, by being the breadwinner)." This would miss Paul's whole point. What he's really saying is "Husbands, you surely love yourselves. For instance, you take proper care of your bodies by feeding and clothing them. So, too, you should give all love and care for your wives, doing *whatever* is necessary to this end." In many situations this may involve being the breadwinner. In others it may not.

The passages that list the qualifications for the office of elder (1 Timothy 3:1-7 and Titus 1:6-9) shed no light on the issue. In 1 Timothy 3:4*a* Paul does say that an elder "must manage his own family well." But, as the context makes clear, Paul is not trying to teach anything about an elder's fiscal responsibility to his family. Rather, he's talking about his success at discipline. That is clear from the last half of the verse, which reads, "and see that his children obey him with proper respect."

Paul's point is simply that the family is the proving ground for an elder. He must have shown that he can control his own children before he has a right to oversee a whole congregation. This has no direct bearing on his role as breadwinner.

These passages, then, shed little light on the topic. What does the rest of the Bible tell us?

As we examine the Old Testament, we find sloth roundly condemned. Proverbs especially makes some pretty biting remarks about the sluggard. For instance, Proverbs 19:24: "The sluggard buries his hand in the dish; he will not even bring it back to his mouth!" These comments apply equally to men and women.

Almost nothing, however, deals directly with the question, "Who should be the family's breadwinner?" At first I was rather perplexed with this. Why did God give His covenant people so little instruction on such an important topic? One day the answer hit me: The issue wasn't even relevant to Israelite society.

Think for a moment about life in ancient Israel. Its people lived in small towns and villages. They farmed plots of ground in the fields around their town or tended flocks in the nearby pastures. Sometimes, husband and wife may have worked side by side. At other times, they probably did different tasks. Perhaps the man drove the team of oxen (hard physical work) or threshed the grain, while his wife went to the market to sell the produce. The children, meanwhile, spent part of their time helping their father in the field, the rest with their mother in the market. The whole issue of the father "going out to work" and the mother "staying home to rear the kids" didn't arise; and it still isn't relevant today in primarily agrarian societies.

*I*n Proverbs 31 we have a description of a woman who is a diligent merchant and entrepreneur. . . . In a phrase, she's running a family business.

Despite the absence of specific teaching on the issue, the Old Testament does offer an occasional glimpse into the role of husband and wife in ancient Israel. One passage is particularly revealing—namely, the last half of Proverbs 31, sometimes entitled "The Wife of Noble Character." Please note in particular verses 15-18, where the woman who is earlier said to bring her husband "good, not harm, all the days of his life" (v. 12) "gets up while it is still dark." The description is impressive:

> she provides food for her family
> and portions for her servant girls.
> She considers a field and buys it;
>   out of her earnings she plants a vineyard.
> She sets about her work vigorously;
>   her arms are strong for her tasks.
> She sees that her trading is profitable,
>   and her lamp does not go out at night.

Here we have a description of a woman who is a diligent merchant and entrepreneur, apparently able to earn sufficient money to buy land that she will then work to increase her profits. In a phrase, she's running a family business.

And what is her husband doing? We're not told much, other than what we read in verse 23: "Her husband is respected at the city gate, where he takes his seat among the elders of the land."

The elders of the gate adjudicated disputes, much like judges do today. If not a full-time occupation, it was certainly time-consuming and probably without financial compensation. A man in this position would be greatly aided by a spouse who could contribute substantially to the needs of their household.

When we turn to the New Testament, certain comments appear directly relevant, and on first reading seem to teach that the husband should be out working while the wife stays at home. Three crucial passages are 2 Thessalonians 3:10-12; 1 Timothy 5:8; and Titus 2:5. The first of these says,

> For even when we were with you, we gave you this rule: "If a man will not work, he shall not eat." We hear that some among you are idle. They are not busy, they are busybodies. Such people we command and urge in the Lord Jesus Christ, to settle down and earn the bread they eat.

This passage appears to instruct husbands to provide income for themselves and their families through their work. However, the Greek word translated *man* in verse 10 is *tis*. This word can be either masculine or feminine and corresponds most closely to our English word *anyone*. (This is how the King James Version translates it.) Moreover, in the Greek the phrase translated "he shall not eat" can have either a masculine or feminine pronoun as subject. A more literal and accurate translation would be: "If anyone will not work, let that person not eat."

---

*P*aul's comments *[in 2 Thessa-lonians 3:10-12] are a general warning against idleness and not a command given specifically to men.*

Paul's comments, then, are a general warning against idleness and not a command given specifically to men. They do not support the contention that husbands should be the primary breadwinner.

In 1 Timothy 5:8 we read, "If anyone does not provide for his relatives, and especially for his immediate family, he has denied the faith and is worse than an infidel."

Once again, the Greek word is *tis*, and it's impossible to tell from the Greek whether Paul is addressing his comments to men alone or to men and women alike. But let's suppose he is addressing men as heads of households. It doesn't follow that he is telling them to go out to work. All he is saying is that as the heads of households they have a duty to see that their family and relatives are provided for. This *may* require going out to work. Circumstances vary, however. Perhaps the husband is prevented from being the family's breadwinner. Or it may be more feasible for his wife to fulfill this role. Paul is simply telling men to make sure that their families have what they need. How this is accomplished is secondary.

Finally, there is Titus 2:5. We will consider the verse in its context by quoting verses 3-5:

> Likewise, teach the older women to be reverent in the way they live, not to be slanderers or addicted to much wine, but to teach what is good. Then they can train the younger women to love their husbands and children, to be self-controlled and pure, to be busy at home, to be kind, and to be subject to their husbands, so that no one will malign the word of God.

The crucial statement is that women should be "busy at home." Is Paul's purpose to tell women to stay at home or to stay busy while at home? In other words, is Paul saying, "Women are to be at *home* working" or "Women are to be at home *working*"?

Just as the Old Testament must be read in the context of agrarian Israel, Paul's letters must be placed in the context in which he was writing. Titus, to whom Paul wrote this epistle, was living among Cretans. The island of Crete was part of a fairly urbanized Greek society. In that culture, many men worked outside the house and their wives stayed at home to rear the family. There was no ancient Greek equivalent to Met Life Insurance, where a woman could work as a file clerk, a secretary, or even an executive. Since a Cretan woman would have had little opportunity to work outside the house, Paul would have had no reason to make this comment had he simply wanted women to stay at home. This was already assured by the mores of Greek society.

It seems much more plausible, then, that Paul, knowing that Cretan women would be at home in any case, is telling them to stay busy. In other words, "Don't be idle. Accept your role and do your housework diligently." To read anything more into Paul's remark is to create a norm out of a cultural variable.

The Bible ... frequently warns against laziness by the husband. However, there is little biblical support for the idea that the husband is shirking his duty if the wife is the primary breadwinner.

Let's sum up. First, the Bible teaches male headship in the family and frequently warns against laziness by the husband. However, there is little biblical support for the idea that the husband is shirking his duty if the wife is the primary breadwinner. The only Old Testament passage that provides much insight (Proverbs 31) runs contrary to this. Moreover, the New Testament passages that may appear to teach this are either gender-neutral (2 Thessalonians 3:10-12; 1 Timothy 5:8) or are easily explained in terms of the cultural context (Titus 2:5).

Therefore, we may conclude that there is nothing in itself unbiblical about a situation where the wife is out working and the husband is keeping the home fires burning.

In closing, I'd like to issue some disclaimers. Above all, I am not endorsing that husband and wife both join the work force and farm out their children to day care or baby-sitters. Children, particularly those of preschool age, need the nurture and care that can only be given by a parent. There may be times when husband and wife must both work to provide the basics. But altogether too often the primary motivation behind the two-income family is the simultaneous advancement of two careers or the maintenance of a more comfortable lifestyle. Our children are more important than our careers, a vacation home, or a fancy sports car. Whether it's Mom or Dad, someone needs to be home caring for the children.

Nor am I advocating a wholesale shift in the roles traditionally performed by husbands and wives. I'm not saying, "Wives, go out and get a job! Husbands, stay at home!" There may be very good reasons that most husbands should be the breadwinners and their wives the caretakers of the children and the home.

However, there are times when this will not or cannot be. Perhaps the husband loses his job and faces long-term unemployment. Maybe a debilitating illness or injury keeps him at home. Perhaps his own skills are valued far less by society than his wife's and as a simple economic proposition it makes more sense for his wife to be working. Maybe his special gifts can best be used in God's kingdom on a full-time but unpaid basis. Possibly even his temperament may be better suited than his wife's to staying home and caring for the children.

For all those husbands and wives who find themselves in this situation but want to maintain a biblical lifestyle, I hope I've provided comfort. God's Word does not condemn you.

A Working Mother's Memoirs

by Elizabeth Erlandson

*L*eaving my children and going out to work was the last thing I ever planned to do.

I was proud of being a stay-at-home mom. And I really believed that was the way things had to be for a family to be truly in God's will. So when it became apparent that things weren't working out in the pastorate and that the Lord wasn't opening another position for Doug, we began to talk about the possibility of my going out to work for a while. But as far as I was concerned, that's all it was—talk.

In reality, God was preparing us for a major change. And although that change involved my getting a job that in other circumstances I might have embraced, the very thought of becoming a working mother was galling, humbling, and a trial that threatened to tear my soul apart. I felt cheated.

The first week on the job was awful. I missed my children. I was sure that something terrible would happen to them, now that I wasn't around to protect them. I was also convinced that I'd fail as a professional public relations writer. And I couldn't imagine how we would make ends meet with greater expenses and a smaller income.

T he thought of becoming a working mother was galling, humbling, and a trial that threatened to tear my soul apart.

Thankfully I had a private office where I could close the door and cry. And that's exactly what I did. I could barely pray for myself, but God did not abandon me. Halfway into the first week, I received a phone call from an editor with whom I had worked when I was a free-lance writer. A widow rearing two children, Sandra had endured much greater disappointment than I. She listened as I poured out my humiliation. She said she understood, and I believed her.

Knowing that other women—women who loved God and desired to do His will—also experienced similar fears, frustrations, anger, and sorrow helped me to accept my situation. But that didn't mean that everyone else accepted the idea of my going out to work while Doug stayed home with the children.

I must have been at the job for about a month when a man from another department began talking to me in the cafeteria. He knew little of our situation. He didn't know that Doug had looked for work for two years before we made this switch. He didn't know how much I would have preferred to be at home taking care of my little ones. All he knew was what I had known a few months earlier—*that in godly families, the mother stays home and the father goes to work to provide for his family.*

He made several pointed comments about how he was working two jobs so his wife could stay home with the children. He talked about how they had chosen to live in government housing to reduce their monthly expenses. And he did some quick exegesis of Scripture to make sure that I understood what he was driving at. I felt angry and weak at the end of that conversation. And I determined that, short of wearing a sign that said "I'd rather be home with my kids," I would let everyone know that I was working, not by choice, but because of circumstances beyond our control.

Although I knew that God had led us into this new situation and that He was in control, the reactions of others still hurt. But I prayed that God would use our situation to make me more compassionate of others and less judgmental. I prayed that He would work good out of this difficult development in our lives.

Eventually I adjusted to being away from my children all day. But it wasn't easy or quick. In fact, eighteen months after I began working, I remember feeling immense frustration. Doug was home-schooling Annie, our six year old. *Annie needs me home in the afternoons*, I told myself. *I should be there to play and to help her meet other children in the neighborhood.*

I decided to reduce my schedule to part time at that point, even though it meant a substantial cut in pay and benefits. I took on extra freelance work to make up for the difference.

"Weren't your children angry at you for going to work?" someone asked me recently.

"No, I really don't think so," I answered. "They were disappointed, perhaps, but not angry." And that's true. They missed me a lot at the beginning, so I made sure to limit my other commitments and spend as much time as I could with them in the evenings and on weekends. I snuggled them whenever they wanted, for as long as they wanted. I told them about my work and brought them to the office on several occasions.

---

*M*y attitudes were sinful. . . . I also wanted to blame Doug, silently accusing him of . . . lacking in ambition, of reneging on his responsibilities.

Generally, the children adjusted well. But my own humiliation and frustration at having to work were compounded by the disappointment I felt about Doug's career possibilities. How could God simply set my husband on the shelf? Why would He ignore the wonderful abilities that He had graciously blessed him with? I looked around at other less-talented, less-educated and, as far as I was concerned, less deserving men, and wondered why God had given them position, power, and prestige while

Doug was stuck at home, taking care of the kids, cleaning the house, and making the meals. I hurt for my husband.

As I prayed about our situation, I realized that my attitudes were sinful and that God was dealing with my pride. I also wanted to blame Doug, silently accusing him of having wrong attitudes, of lacking in ambition, of reneging on his responsibilities.

But in my heart, I knew that wasn't true. I knew that God was sovereign and that Doug had done all that he could do. The rest was up to God.

Doug and I continued our practice of having daily devotions as a family. We prayed about our situation. We prayed about our desire for Doug to find a way to bring in money, while caring for the children. We prayed that God would open doors for Doug to minister. Most of all, we prayed that we would accept God's will for our lives and glorify Him in this situation.

God did open doors. Slowly, but surely, He made a straight path for our feet. Things have changed. Things are better.

Best of all, *we* have changed. We are different people today. I like to think that we are better people, having trusted God as He led us through a job crisis as part of His perfect plan.

NOTES

1. These and many other fascinating career changes are described by Rochelle Jones in *The Big Switch* (New York: McGraw-Hill, 1980).
2. For the sake of simplicity I have not considered an itemized return. Obviously, the exact differential will depend on how many deductions are declared. The differential, however, will be close to or the same as it is on a nonitemized return.
3. The reason the differential doesn't stand at $4,000 is because a family with an adjusted gross income of $25,000 is going to pay more in income tax and Social Security than will a family with an income of $20,000. So the smaller differential with which we start is partially offset by smaller subtractions for income and Social Security taxes.
4. For further guidance on reentering the work force, refer to the books listed at the end of chapter 4. Many have chapters devoted to the issue of women reentering the job market. Some also show how to construct a functional résumé.
5. Bernard Asbell, with Karen Wynn, "What They Know About You," *The Old Farmer's Almanac* (Dublin, N.H.: Yankee, 1992), p. 95.
6. The basic information contained in this dictionary may be found in Betty Michelozzi, *Coming Alive from Nine to Five*, 3d edition (Mountain View, Calif.: Mayfield, 1988).
7. David K. Eyler, *Starting and Operating a Home-based Business* (New York: John Wiley & Sons, 1990), p. 10. This number is probably somewhat low. It is based on the number of people who file tax returns for such businesses. There are others who operate on a strictly cash basis and who fail to file returns and have so far escaped detection by the IRS. Their number is impossible to accurately estimate.
8. Eyler, *Starting and Operating*, p. 10.
9. The information on the productivity of telecommuters is from Lis Fleming, *The One-Minute Commuter* (Davis, Calif.: Acacia, 1989), p. 46. My belief that the self-employed are even more productive is based on the fact that because they are working for themselves and their income is largely dependent on how much they produce, they are likely to work even harder and more efficiently than the telecommuter.
10. The number of new people a program of this sort will bring into a church will vary from one situation to another and will depend on a variety of factors. The number given for Oak Lake represents an average for churches that have begun similar programs.

Moody Press, a ministry of the Moody Bible Institute,
is designed for education, evangelization, and edification.
If we may assist you in knowing more about Christ
and the Christian life, please write us without obligation:
Moody Press, c/o MLM, Chicago, Illinois 60610.